THE WOMEN

OF THE ENGLISH CIVIL WAR

by

Margaret Cooper Evans

First published 2015

Nuova Stella

First published 2015 by Nuova Stella (Publishing)

Cover by Andrew Evans

ISBN 978-0-9934068-0-5

This is a historical work. All the characters and events portrayed in this book existed and have been fully researched.

Many of the anecdotes mentioned in the book have been related to me by the families of those involved themselves; their House Guides, representatives or local people. I take no responsibility for the accuracy of information gathered in this way.

All the photographs in this book have been taken by myself or my husband Andrew Evans and copyright of such belongs to ourselves.

All other images used have been checked as out of copyright or free to use. Attributions can be found at the end of the book.

This history book is unusual as I speak through it, mentioning my own views on the events. These are my views only and not the views of any other organisation or person other than myself.

Other Books by
MARGARET COOPER-EVANS

FICTION
The Hilary Long Mysteries
Upside down in Overdown
Summertime in Overdown
Christmastime in Overdown
Man Down in Overdown

(in production for Christmas 2015)
The Hilary Long Mysteries Collection
Halloween in Overdown

also
Jago, part one of the Carter Trilogy.

Available to buy from the Kindle Store

With thanks to

The Sealed Knot re-enactment Society
The Women Re-enactors of the Sealed Knot
The National Trust Claydon House & Chastleton House
Lord Ingilby of Ripley Castle
The Ashmolean Museum, Oxford
Basing House, Hampshire
Lord & Lady Sele & Seye Broughton Castle
Cromwell's House, Ely
English Heritage, Bolsover Castle
The Newark Civil War Museum
and
The Women of the English Civil War without whom this book would not exist

Table of Contents

Table of Contents

Introduction

Forget everything you think you know about women during the English Civil War. Spies, soldiers, scientists, the women of the 17th Century were all these and more. Thrown into a turbulent new world with a war that split families apart and had them fighting on different sides. These are the forgotten stories of bravery and audacity of women from all walks of life, who protected their livelihoods, homes and families during these turbulent times.

Expect the unexpected as throughout this book I hope you will never fail to be surprised at the roads the women take to survive the war. This book doesn't explain all the intricacies of war, but it does explain the intricacies of the lives of the extraordinary women from all classes who lived through it.

My book will tell both sides of the story as the women of England fought against each other to bring peace back to the country they all loved. I hope I can tell their stories and share their hopes, dreams, and achievements alongside a few of their recipes for food, medicine and cosmetics.

Their lives were dictated by the seasons, their food, their clothes, their celebrations. It was something they all knew and understood well.
In January for instance "Fly physic, Sloth and Venery, Avoid all baths most carefully." Neve's Almanack 1633.

It was common sense, keep yourself fit, busy and strong. Winters in the 17th Century were 5 degrees colder than they are now, and you could not catch a cold or you may not survive. Just for information - hands and faces were washed every day!

For marriage and private lives, several self-help manuals were written for young women starting out in life. Outrageous upper-class women like Margaret - Mad Madge - Newcastle married for love, but most marriages were arranged and love (or hate) grew over the years. In these manuals, like today's self help books, there was everything you needed to know; from how to keep your husband, "keep yourself to your wifely duties each night, for a man content at home will not wander"; to how to cook and clean and make "physics" (medicines).

After the war a third of the male population of England were dead. Times were hard, pestilence and plague were never far away, and most celebrations were banned by the new Commonwealth. A miserable end to what had been a momentous time for the women of England who had fought and lived so bravely through it. I discovered that around sixteen thousand women died during the English Civil War, and that is no small number.

Reading any modern accounts of the English Civil Wars, all you will generally find at the front of the book will be a list of battles in one column and in the next column a list of the men's names that were in charge of them.

It's almost as if the women didn't exist and didn't live through the same upheavals of the time that the men did. In short the modern male historian has sidelined women. Even in the re-enactment societies of today, the women's role in the action has been marginalised, undervalued, and yet they still fight on.

Throughout the Civil Wars, the women stood up to be counted among the men. They fought and died with them, as foot soldiers, musketeers, colonels, and siege matrons. We must not forget the other women who made a considerable contribution to the soldier's way of life, the Baggage women who cooked, fed and nursed them, and of course, their whores.

It is for all those wonderful forgotten women, who fought bravely, lived on their wits, and out manoeuvred the opposition that I write this book.

Margaret Cooper Evans

Timeline of the Women's War

1625

11th May King Charles marries Henrietta Maria by proxy at the Notre Dam in Paris.
Henrietta is 15 years old.
Henrietta Maria arrives in England and is met by Charles.

1626

2nd February Charles is crowned as King.
Henrietta is not crowned as a Queen and never will be as she is a Catholic.
13th June Henrietta Maria is married to Charles in St Augustine's Church, Canterbury, Kent.

1640/41

3rd November The Long Parliament meets.
22nd March Trial of the Earl of Strafford known as Tyrant Tom.
The Queen attends the trial of Strafford to support her husband.
12th May The Earl of Strafford executed.

1642

5th March The Queen goes to Holland to deliver her 10 year old daughter Mary to William of Orange as his bride, but is also going to sell the crown jewels and to raise money for arms.
22nd August The King raises his standard at Nottingham signalling the official start of war.
23rd October Battle of Edgehill, Royalist advantage.

1643

22nd February The Queen lands at Bridlington and is attacked by Parliamentary forces.
1st May Mary Bankes defends the first Parliament attack on Corfe Castle.
23rd May The Queen is impeached by the Commons.
23rd June The Siege of Corfe Castle begins in earnest and Mary Bankes requests help from Royalist forces.
25th July The siege of Brampton Bryan begins and Lady Brilliana Harley repels the Royalist attack.
4th August Mary Bankes fights for her home, Corfe Castle.

31st October Brilliana Harley dies a broken woman from the stress,
her castle is ruined and her lands laid waste.
6-13 November William Waller attacks Basing House allowing the Marchioness free passage to leave before the assault as she was the half sister to Parliament's Earl of Essex.

1644

26th January Battle of Nantwich. 120 women, believed to be a cruel Irish Regiment with long knives, are taken into custody.
27th February Lady Charlotte Strange refuses to give up Lathom House to Parliament or make any concessions to them, the siege of Lathom house begins.
29th March The Battle of Cheriton.
18th May The marriage of Anne Harrison to Richard Fanshaw starting their diplomatic career together.
16th June The Queen gives birth to Princess Henrietta Anne.
29th June Battle of Cropedy Bridge.
2nd July Battle of Marston Moor.
10th July The Queen sails from Falmouth.
The crossing is so bad she and her ladies have to be cut from their salt and vomit encrusted clothes on arrival at their destination.
11th July The siege of Basing House begins, a waiting woman and a chambermaid are killed by the bombardment.

1645

January Abortive peace talks take place.
February Siege of Scarborough Castle.
April Formation of the New Model Army.
20th May Anne Fanshaw joins her husband and the Prince of Wales in Bristol.
14th June Battle of Naseby
Over a 100 women of quality killed and robbed. The baggage women and whores had their noses slit as punishment.
10th July Battle of Langport.
21st August Basing House pounded into rubble by Col Dalbier's batteries bringing down one tower so effectively that household goods fell into the yard.
10th September Prince Rupert surrenders Bristol
8th October Cromwell arrives at Basing House bringing heavy artillery with him.
Miss Griffiths trying to protect her father, a rector, had her brains dashed out.
Other women were stripped naked and "entertained" by common soldiers.
16th October Nothing remains of Basing but the cellars and a few bare walls,
Cromwell moves on leaving his injured men to die in the burning cellars.
December Lathom House surrenders.

1646

27th February Mary Bankes hands over the keys to Corfe Castle and watches as her much loved home is looted and destroyed.
5th May The King surrenders to the Scots at Newark, this brings about the end of the first Civil War.
25th June The Prince of Wales leaves for France.
25th July Lady Dalkieth escapes to France with Princess Henrietta Ann.

1647

30th January The Scots hand the King over to Parliament.
4th June The King is removed from Holdenby Hall.
11th November At Hampton Court, the King is visited by Jane Whorwood his spy. She advises him, with the help of an astrologer, to go into hiding in Essex. Instead the King escapes from Hampton Court and travels to the Isle of Wight mistakenly believing he has a friend in the Governor there, he becomes a prisoner in Carisbrooke Castle.
26th December The king signs an engagement with the Scots.

1648

20th April The Duke of York escapes to Holland disguised as a young woman with the help of Anne Murray.

1649

20th January The King's trial begins.
27th January The King is sentenced to death.
30th January The King is executed in Whitehall, Jane Whorwood presses through the crowds to say her goodbyes, encouraging the rumours that they were lovers.

Two weeks later Queen Henrietta Maria is told of the death of her husband. The Queen at first refuses to believe it, thinking that he must have escaped, by being rescued from the scaffold by a mob of loyal Londoners.
When the truth sinks in she stands motionless and in silence
for a whole afternoon, only crying when her sister in law comes to offer her condolences.

The Road to War

Getting ready to march off to War.(i)

Charles I inherited a bankrupt kingdom from his father James. Not only had James helped fund the Thirty Years War in Holland which cost him dearly, he also led a corrupt and profligate lifestyle. He kept two courts: one for himself and his young men; and one for his wife Anne of Denmark.

It was a different story when James I of Scotland inherited Elizabeth I's England. He inherited full coffers and a land that had been at peace for nearly 30 years. He managed to work his way through all her gold and jewels, even having the pearls and precious jewels cut from her dresses. His wife Anne of Denmark sent her friends Elizabeth's elaborate and bejewelled stomachers and shifts as expensive presents.

Despite his predilection for handsome young men, James managed to father eight children with Anne, only three of whom survived; Henry, Charles and Elizabeth.

Charles was not meant to be King or trained for it. His older brother Henry, was handsome, charismatic, athletic, and well educated. This popular young man was to be the next King. He was not so popular with Charles as he used to bully him, making fun of his rickety legs and telling him that when he became King he would make Charles a bishop, so the long cloak he had to wear would hide them. Charles burst into tears and had to be dragged away. However, this was not to be. The arrogant Henry died at the age of 18 from TB, leaving Charles as the sole heir to his father's throne.

Charles was short because of his damaged legs. He also had a stutter that he fought hard all his life to overcome, none the less he took on the mantle of the monarchy and with it the Divine Right of Kings. Charles believed he had been chosen by God to be the King of England, and he was going to rule England. When Parliament disagreed with him, he decided he no longer needed it and disbanded it to rule on his own.

Others always easily influenced Charles throughout his life. He never really had the courage of his own convictions. He swayed to and fro with decisions until others took it out of his hands and unfortunately, when he did decide to do something on the spur of the moment, it was usually a mistake.

On his father's death, as well as the Crown, Charles also inherited his father's lover, George Villiers, as his advisor. The beautiful and corrupt Duke of Buckingham was known affectionately by father and son as *"Steenie".

George Villiers hoped to exert the same influence over Charles as he did his father. He was instrumental in pushing Henrietta Maria away and causing trouble between the new husband and his new French wife.

** The Duke of Buckingham was known as "Steenie", named after the Leonardo da Vinci portrait of St Steven, whom he painted as a beautiful young man.*

It was The Duke of Buckingham who escorted Charles to Spain in an abortive attempt to win the hand of the Spanish Princess, and was by his side when Charles met Henrietta Maria for the first time. Perhaps the relationship was that of the younger man looking up to an older brother figure, although some historians have suggested it might have been more than that. Whatever the relationship was between the two men, Henrietta Maria found herself isolated and alone. Her Catholic Court had been depleted by Buckingham's influence on the King.

The Duke of Buckingham lived expensively and dressed expensively, famously even having diamonds in the feathers of his cap. He cared more for his own image than for England and his King, they were just a means to an end. On the 23rd August 1628 he was in a public house in Portsmouth called The Greyhound. He was preparing for another ill-fated raid on La Rochelle, when John Felton, an army officer who had been wounded in the earlier siege of the Ille de Rhe, ran into the inn and stabbed him to death.

John Felton unknowingly changed many women's lives that day. Henrietta Maria's, Hester Tradescant, Buckingham's own faithful wife Katherine, and the wives of the men who were due to depart with his Lordship on a siege that was likely to be as disastrous as all his others.

Buckingham was universally hated in England and it was with great relief that the mercenaries, pressed men and other combatants left for their wives, children and homes.

John Felton gave himself up, Buckingham was the most hated man in England at the time, and he didn't believe that he would be arrested. He was expecting to be applauded for his actions and actually admitted to the assassination. He was arrested immediately and taken to the Magistrates court.

While awaiting trial, Lieutenant John Felton had poems written about his assassination of the Duke.

"The Duke is dead, and we are rid of strife
by Felton's hand that took away his life
A rotten member, that can have no cure,
Must be cut off to save the body sure"

John Felton walked to his death by hanging at Tyburn on 29th November 1628, for the murder of the Duke of Buckingham. In his hat were the written statements he had carried to the assassination. After his death these were widely circulated. Anyone praising Felton for his actions, lived in fear of having their ears cut off and being fined. John Felton's body was sent back to Portsmouth to be exhibited as a lesson to others but instead of becoming a warning, it was venerated by a grateful public.

Lady Katherine on advice went into hiding, but Henrietta Maria had another battle to win, that of her husband's love. It was said that Charles cried for days and shut himself away to pray for Buckingham's soul.

Charles seemed inconsolable. Henrietta gently comforted him, although it must have been galling for her, she did not criticise or praise his precious "Steenie", she gradually won Charles over. The King fell in love with his patient and pretty little Queen and she with him. They re-started their journey together as affectionate and loving as newly-weds should be. Henrietta very quickly became pregnant and in 1629 after a difficult childbirth they lost their first child, a year later in 1630 when she gave birth to Charles II, their happiness was complete.

Henrietta took over from the Duke of Buckingham as Charles closest friend and advisor and supported him throughout the Civil War.

Charles could no longer endure Parliament's censures and when he imposed the Ship Tax without the consent of Parliament it was the one of the King's many actions that helped to push the country into civil war.

The war started in earnest on the 22nd August 1642, when Charles raised his standard at Nottingham.

The England of 1642 was not prepared for war. August in England was Harvest time, men were sweating - working in the fields, and women were brewing beer and making drinks containing Hyssop and white wine to stop the workers falling asleep from heat exhaustion amongst the corn stacks.

There was hardly an Army left, the military all but forgotten. Many towns had no longer repaired or renewed their fortifications, and no one expected to be fighting a war again, least of all against their own countrymen.

Families were divided by the war, like the Verneys. The son Ralph was a Parliamentarian and the father Edmund, bravely fought and died for the King. The women of the Verney family became the prey of both sides of the sword divided.

So it began, the usual quiet-ish life of the hearth and home were to become things of the past for many women. In the August sunshine in their cool stone kitchens, making tansy water for the sore and smelly feet of their men, little did they know what terrors lay ahead for some of them and what adventures others of them might have. One thing they all knew from both sides was that whatever the outcome, their world would be turned upside down, as in the popular broadside ballad and nothing would ever be the same again.

These are the first few lines of the popular song The World turned Upside Down. It was written in the middle of the 1640s as a protest against the policies of Parliament, who cancelled Christmas and outlawed traditional English Christmas celebrations. There are several versions of the lyrics. It is sung to the tune of another ballad, "When the King Enjoys his own again."

The whole of the Ballad is printed at the end of the book, it's quite long, but the tune is bouncy and jolly, the words witty and political, everything the Parliamentarians would not like to hear.

The World Turned Upside Down

A broadside ballad written after the English Civil War that describes how life changed for the people of England.

Listen to me and you shall hear,
news hath not been this thousand year:
Since Herod, Caesar, and many more,
you never heard the like before.
Holy-dayes are despis'd, new fashions are devis'd.
Old Christmas is kicked out of Town

Yet let's be content, and the times lament,
you see the world turn'd upside down.

The poor old cook, in the larder doth look,
Where is no goodnesse to be found,

Yet let's be content, and the times lament,
you see the world turn'd upside down.

To conclude, I'll tell you news that's right,
Christmas was kil'd at Naseby fight.

Women of the English Civil Wars

Can you tell the women from the men in this photo? (ii)

A mother on horseback with two pistols aimed at her own son to stop him trying to land his army from a ship. A forty year old spinster holding a seasoned army commander prisoner in a library after she had been fighting all day on horseback. A widow trying to steal the Kings jewels and going on the run to Wales. An escape attempt made by putting a file in a cake (for the very first time) by a red haired female spy. A queen running back to pick up her lapdog whilst being fired on by snipers.

Any of this familiar? No?

I have been writing and researching for my book about Women in the English Civil War for the past twenty years. It started when I became a Sealed Knot re-enactor, women were being largely sidelined and I thought they must have taken more part in the war than the usual whores, baggage train, or camp followers that were being re-enacted.

The more I researched the more the women came to life from the past shouting to be heard after 370 years of neglect.

I would like to think that this book would appeal to everyone with an interest in history, The English Civil Wars, costume, food, medical treatment, weaponry, re-enactment, also women's position in society past and present. It would give modern day people a view into the past that had never been seen before.

How could a woman fight as a man and not get found out? As it happens with a hand-made leather penis so she could relieve herself against a tree with the other troops. This woman was so successful dressed as a man, that she was accused by a local whore of fathering a child and paid for it to be brought up rather than be found out so she could stay in the army with her husband.

During the English Civil War women stepped out of the confines of hearth and home and into battle, many modern women are doing the same today. Some for real and some as re-enactors.

This book is dedicated to the women of the Sealed Knot. Thank you for all your help, fun and companionship over the years.

Queen Henrietta-Maria

Henrietta-Maria as a young woman. (iii)

In 1625 at the age of fifteen a small girl, young for her age, stood in the Notre Dam in Paris. She was about to marry by proxy, Charles I of England. Pretty with dark curled hair and an oval face, Henrietta Maria waited for the service to start. Charles' stand in was to be his best friend The Duke of Buckingham. He had charmed and infuriated the French Court in equal measure during the negotiations for Henrietta-Maria's hand by wearing extravagantly bejewelled clothes and trying to bed a royal lady - Anne of Austria -but fate took a hand in the arrangements.

Charles' father James, had just died, it meant that none of the English court could attend the wedding. So dressed in black mourning clothes and wearing a red bejewelled scarf, the Duc de Chevreuse stood next to the little girl, as the stand in for them both.

In 1626 Henrietta-Maria met her husband for the first time on English soil at Dover in Kent. In her keeping was a letter from her mother, Marie de Medici, giving her advice on how to run a Royal household. She was also told to promote her Catholic faith, which many thought the true reason for her marriage. It was a big remit for a sixteen year old girl.

She was accompanied by her own court ladies, and Buckingham's sister, mother, and niece with their translator, the Catholic Sir Toby Matthew. The Buckingham ladies had been sent to her as her English ladies in waiting. At this time Henrietta-Maria spoke no English, she had been trying to learn but found it difficult.
Apart from her boxes of clothes and jewels, her large retinue also included her lap-dogs, her priest and her friend Madame Mamie St George.

Little did she know that she was about to start the adventure of a lifetime. The shy quiet little King with a stutter did not promise as much, but she was to come into her own as his valued aide de camp, and become known as “she majesty Generalissima”.

After the wedding night, Henrietta-Maria was reported as suffering from green sickness (her periods) but was told the cure for this was her new husband! Charles however was very happy and slept late - until 7am!

Charles and Henrietta-Maria were forced to share the coach with the Buckingham ladies. This left no room for Henrietta- Maria's best friend and companion, Madame St George. As they made their way through the cheering crowds in London, Henrietta felt upset by this and later, the French Court felt themselves insulted. As it was early days nothing was said officially, but later on the flight from the plague in London, it was apparently the cause of the couples' first argument in private. It was then

Charles realised that he had married a woman who knew her own mind and who was no pushover, he wasn't pleased at this discovery. Charles spoke fluent French so they had no problem communicating and he knew exactly what she was saying to him.

It was obvious to everyone that Charles and Henrietta were affectionate towards each other during their honeymoon period. As a romantic Charles showed his Henrietta London from the top of the Tower of London, and cannons boomed in celebration of the new Queen of England, it seemed all would be well for the newly-weds.

However, London was in the grip of an outbreak of plague, with more and more people dying every day, so the King and his new bride moved swiftly to the cleaner air of Hampton Court.

The one fly in this perfumed ointment, was the Duke of Buckingham, nothing was done in the King's Court without his say so. He tried to influence the new Queen by trying to appoint the Buckingham ladies to all the important positions in her court. This was rejected and an angry Buckingham complained bitterly to the Queen, but the French would have none of it and set themselves against the interfering Duke.

Henrietta-Maria could see that Buckingham was going to make her life with Charles difficult. She was moved from Palace to Palace to avoid the ravages of the plague, during this time she was reminded by her French advisors of her part of the marriage contract, to stop the persecution of Catholics in England.

On the way to Oxford, Henrietta brought the subject up, but Charles told her he couldn't do what she asked. Although Catholic toleration was part of the wedding contract, Parliament would not agree to fund Charles' war unless the anti-Catholic laws were upheld.

Even Henrietta-Maria herself was affected by this, although she was called the Queen in name, she would never be crowned because she was a Catholic. She soon found that Charles' promises were not going to be made good. He was more interested in the money the marriage brought to the

Crown to help pay off his father's debts and start a war under Buckingham's influence.

Charles became obsessed with the loss of his father, he had the ceiling at Whitehall Palace painted to honour him, the divine right of Kings, up in Heaven with God and the Angels.

Charles did not see the true man who was profligate with the Crown's purse. James liked spending it on his lovers, especially his favourite, the Duke of Buckingham calling him "Steenie" and "my dear dogge", and worst of all signing his love letters to him, "my sweet child and wife, and grant that ye may ever be a comfort to your dear dad and husband."

He gave his wife, Anne of Denmark, her own court to keep her out of his way. Filled his own court with pretty young men, some dressed as women for appearances sake, and yet he was so hypocritical that he wrote a treatise on the evils of sodomy.
But Charles saw his father differently, and nothing would sway his opinion of him.

Throughout this time Henrietta-Maria was forced to endure constant barracking from the Duke of Buckingham. It was said that George Villiers entered the Queen's chambers more than the King did. He even came late at night to tell her off for the things he thought she'd done wrong.

> *"The King is displeased with you, he tells me his servants exercise their marital rights more than he does."*

Perhaps if Buckingham had stood out of the way, the King and Queen could have made their lives together properly, sharing a bed and confidences with each other without the aid of a third party. Instead they spent their time quarrelling whenever they met.

George Villiers had managed to keep them apart for six weeks at this time, so that he had the King's ear to himself.

The beautiful but corrupt George Villiers, the Duke of Buckingham the most hated man in England in 1625 (iv)

Life changed for Henrietta-Maria when another life ended.

On the 23rd August 1628 the Duke of Buckingham had just finished breakfast in the Greyhound Inn, a local public house in Portsmouth. He was about to leave to prepare for another ill-fated raid on La Rochelle when suddenly John Felton, an army officer who had been wounded in the earlier siege of the Ille de Rhe, ran into the inn and stabbed George Villiers through the heart. John Felton's family had starved to death while he was fighting for Buckingham. He had been promised compensation for his wounds and his work. It was not forthcoming and he found his wife and child dead on return to his home. No neighbours had come forward to help them.

Buckingham's wife Katherine was at the Greyhound Inn at the time, she was distraught screaming for help. John Felton unknowingly changed many women's lives that day. Henrietta Marias', Buckingham's own faithful wife, Katherine,and the wives of the men due to depart with his Lordship on a siege that was likely to be as disastrous as all his others. His Cadiz expedition took the lives of 7000 Englishmen. Buckingham was only saved from being imprisoned by Parliament for corruption and incompetence by Charles's intervention.

Buckingham was universally hated in England and it was with great relief that the mercenaries, pressed men and other combatants left for their wives, children and homes.

John Felton gave himself up, possibly believing that he would not be charged for his crime. However he was arrested and hanged at Tyburn on 29th November 1628.The authorities sent his body was sent back to Portsmouth as a lesson to others but instead of becoming a warning, it was venerated.

Lady Katherine on advice went into hiding, but Henrietta Maria had another battle to win, that of her husband's love. It was said that Charles cried for days and shut himself away to pray for Buckingham's soul. Buckingham was buried in Westminster Abbey, at night. He was so hated it was thought he would be dug up and desecrated and his head would be put on a pike somewhere. There is a rumour that the body buried in Westminster Abbey that night was not that of Buckingham.

The King did not seem to notice the "extraordinary joy" of his people who drank the health of Buckingham's murderer and lit bonfires of rejoicing, he shut himself away in his room sobbing.

Charles seemed inconsolable. Henrietta gently comforted him, although it must have been galling for her, she did not criticise or praise his precious *"Steenie". She gradually won Charles over, King fell in love with his patient and pretty little Queen again and she with him.

They re-started their journey together as affectionate and loving as newly-weds should be. Henrietta very quickly became pregnant and in 1629 after a difficult childbirth where a surgeon, Dr Chamberlen was called to help. "Your wife or child Sire?" He had asked Charles, Charles chose Henrietta, they could have other children, but she had become irreplaceable to him. The child, a boy, was born alive, but died within an hour, shortly after being christened.

A year later on Friday 28th May when the Queen gave birth to Charles II they were both overjoyed. They had spent the year together very much in each other's company, and Charles delighted in having such a happy marriage, regretting the times he had to leave Henrietta-Maria to attend to affairs of state.

Unfortunately, the start of the English Civil War was bubbling up just under the horizon, and a whole new set of adventures were about to upset the happy couple's apple-cart.

In 1642 the King raised his standard at Nottingham at the start of the English Civil War. Life for Henrietta-Maria and her children would never be the same again.

On the 23rd of February 1642 Queen Henrietta-Maria and her daughter, the ten year old Princess Mary, were leaving Dover for Holland. The King had come to the harbour to say his goodbyes and kissed them both, he held his little Queen to him tightly, both were in tears, probably wondering if they would see each other again.

Princess Mary had been married at the age of nine to Prince William of Orange, and it was generally thought that the Queen was taking her daughter to live with her new family until the marriage proper could take place. The real reasons were that Henrietta-Maria as a Catholic had lived under threat of impeachment for the past fifteen months and was being sent to a place of safety and to pawn or sell the Crown Jewels in Holland to fund the war.

At the age of thirty two, Henrietta was exhausted, she had borne Charles ten children, and lived under the stress of the oncoming war for two years. When her niece Sophie met her for the first time she describes her as

> *"a thin little woman with long lean arms and teeth protruding from her mouth like guns from a fort."*

Sophie was eleven, with an eleven year old's take on the world,
at that age no-one is perfect. Van Dycks portraits of the Queen may be flattering and they certainly don't show her teeth, which may have been no worse than anyone else's at the time. We may have to believe that a little girls' jealous spite has gone throughout history because she saw a tired

distraught woman and not the glamorous Queen she had been told she was to meet.

During the war Henrietta and Charles wrote to each other in a code called ciphers. In the 17th Century, letters were passed hand to hand by trusted servants and ambassadors. The sender didn't know who opened the letters before they were given to the recipient. Henrietta-Maria was always terrified that their code would be broken and warned the King to keep his cipher on him and not reveal it to anyone.

Henrietta-Maria thought of herself as a good tactician, and often wrote to Charles to tell him what direction she thought he should take. The King was in York, and the Queen wrote to tell him that she he thought he should take Hull before the Parliamentarians did. If the Parliamentarians took the arsenal at Hull before he reached it, he will have lost the war and her efforts in raising money for his fight will have been in vain.

She knew her husband's favourite tactic was to do nothing, so she continually wrote to him, he didn't go to Hull directly but sent his eight year old son James and his nephew Charles Louis. The surprised townspeople accepted them and gave them dinner. However, when they saw Charles and his Cavaliers approaching the town, the reaction was different, and the gates were shut in their faces. I can imagine Henrietta angry with her "I told you so," face on. She wrote to Charles that she wished she had been there to throw the Governor of Hull over the walls and take the town by force.

Instead she turned her attention to trying to buy pistols, carbines, powder and cannon, she also had raised ten thousand pieces. (The money of the day). It was when she was doing this that she heard that the Parliamentarians had taken the arsenal at Hull.

Frustrated and annoyed,she wrote to say she had heard of his "sad loss" and reminded him that if had not delayed in taking Hull he would not have lost his magazine. Also saying

"I am returning to the old point - lose no time, for that will ruin you."

Charles didn't mind the way she spoke to him, it was honest and had his best interests at heart. When she stopped writing for a while, he became worried and wrote

"I would rather have thee chide me than be silent."

Raising money and buying arms was stressful, she also worried about her children, Elizabeth and baby Henry who were now in the hands of Parliament. The Queen developed migraines from crying and writing too much. Parliament realised how much help was coming across the Channel and sent an envoy to tell the Prince of Orange that Dutch ships crossing the channel would be treated as enemy vessels if it continued. Henrietta-Maria was incensed and registered an objection, and to add to her worries she had started to hear rumours that Charles was not happy with her efforts.

She felt this was unfair, and was not prepared to accept that her efforts were in vain. She wrote to say that she had raised thousands of Gilder,200 barrels of powder,3000 muskets and sword, 200 carbines, 3000 pistols and 6 cannon,1000 saddles and pike and wished that those surrounding Charles could have done half as well as she had. If they had Charles would not have been reduced to his present position.

That's the thing with men, when women do things for them, they don't see what women do but point out what they haven't done!

Henrietta wanted to go home, she had sold and pawned everything she had and was now virtually penniless. She left Holland on 2nd February, her fleet of 11 ships put to sea. Parliament ships were on the lookout for them, but the real enemy that day was the weather, one of the worst storms for years blew up across the channel for nine days and nights. The Queen suffered from seasickness and was tied to her bunk, others of her Catholic party were sure they were going to die. Only one person did not suffer seasickness and looked after the rest, a Capuchin Friar, who had been a sailor before he joined the monastery.

They lost two ships and 23 horses but two ships managed to get to Newcastle the rest managed to get back to port in Holland.

For the whole of her life, it must have seemed to Henrietta-Maria that the gods of the sea hated her. She never managed to make a sea journey without incident, and on more than one occasion had to be cut out of her vomit and salt encrusted gowns on her arrival. Still suffering from seasickness, she made arrangements to leave again on the 22nd February, even managing to raise more money in the meantime and getting Parliament ships lying in wait for her warned off. She prayed that God would not put her through this again. He didn't, for once she had a calm crossing and the ships came to rest in Bridlington Bay on the Yorkshire coast. The Queen and her ladies were to be put up in a thatched cottage on the harbour.

I'll let the Queen tell you what happened next in her own words

"That night four Parliament ships arrived without our knowledge,in the morning about four O clock, the alarm was given that we should go down to the harbour and secure our ammunition boats, which had not yet able to be unloaded, but about an hour later these ships began to fire so briskly, that we were all obliged to rise in haste and leave the village to them, at least the women, for the soldiers remained very resolutely to defend the ammunition. One of these ships had done me the favour to flank my house, which fronted the pier, and before I could get out of bed, the balls were whistling upon me in such style that you could not believe I loved not such music. I dressed as it happened as did my ladies..."

Once in the street as her ladies made for ditches to hide in when the Queen realised she had left Mitte her pet dog behind and ran back to fetch her much loved pet. With musket balls whistling round her head she picked up her little dog and she says;

"a serjeant was killed twenty paces from me. We placed ourselves under shelter,(in the ditch) during two hours they were firing upon us, the balls passing over our heads and sometimes covering us with dust."

After the Parliament ships were warned off by the Dutch, the Queen went back to her lodgings,not wanting anyone to say that she had quit the village. Unsurprisingly after her adventure she couldn't sleep or eat very much.

Henrietta-Maria then was to have marched towards Oxford with the Marquess of Newcastle's army, but there was a delay, which frustrated the Queen because she desperately wanted to get back to her husband.

The Marquess had to stop and bury his first wife Elizabeth (nee Bassett), with whom he'd had ten children.

I couldn't find out anything much about Elizabeth's life. Just that her father's name was William, and it was believed they lived in York. But Elizabeth's daughters were writers who wrote a Pastoral (a little play for three sisters) in honour of their father. I imagine Elizabeth to be clever woman who taught her daughters well, and a loving wife who deserved a good burial from her devoted husband. The Queen however, cared for nothing at that time but to get to Charles, her passion to see him overriding any other thoughts or anyone else's needs.

The Queen having been met by his Charle's nephew Prince Rupert of the Rhine was escorted to Stratford on Avon. Where she stayed the night as a guest of Shakepeare's daughter Susanna Hall.

On the 13th July at a village in Oxfordshire called Kineton, just below Edgehill, she was finally re-united with her husband, the King, and her two eldest sons Charles and James.

They stayed the night at Thomas Pope's house in Wroxton and then went on to Woodstock the following day, when they entered Oxford it was in triumph, having heard that the Royalists had won two major victories in the war. The Marquess of Newcastle's army had beaten Fairfaxes, and the Royalist Cavalry had beaten Waller's Horse at Roundway Down.

The Queen established her court in Christchurch College and the King visited her every day after dealing with matters of war. For a year Oxford was the capital of England.

It became the hub of preparation for the next stage of the English Civil War, busy with common soldiers and their women, armourers, and blacksmiths, farriers, every trade associated with war. The hallowed halls of learning became the temporary homes of Lords and Ladies. The town was overcrowded and disease was rife amongst the troops.

The Queen and her court took their exercise in the College gardens, the safest place at the time. She would also listen to music, and hold court, sitting talking ,while her ladies in waiting stood for hours behind her, in their gorgeous silks and jewels to add to her magnificence.

It wasn't long before the war arrived in Oxford and on the 17th of April 1644 the Queen and her retinue left for the West Country.

It was a this time she made an abortive attempt to arrange a marriage between the Prince of Wales and the daughter of the Prince of Orange. She was hoping that by doing this the Dutch would not side with Parliament.

Already pregnant with her ninth child, she decided to go Bath to have the child. The Earl of Essex had marched into the West Country and the heavily pregnant Queen had to move further west to Exeter where she gave birth to a daughter whom she named Henrietta on 16 June.

Unaware that Charle's army were making their way towards her, and frightened that she could be taken hostage, she took a ship from Falmouth on 14 July 1644 and escaped to France leaving her newborn baby behind in the care of a wet nurse. Henrietta-Maria didn't realise that by doing this she would never see her beloved Charles again, if she had not been so impatient they would have been together again in a matter of weeks. When she arrived in France, Henrietta Maria established households at the palace of St Germain and the Louvre with the help of a small stipend from the French government.

She wrote constantly to her husband King Charles, her letters were sometimes full of love and family, and sometimes scheming advising him what he should do in his negotiations with Parliament. All the time using her influence to try and get help for the Royalist cause from the French and the Dutch.

By January 1649 King Charles 1st had been tried and found guilty of being a traitor.

"The said Charles Stuart as a Tyrant, Traitor, Murderer and Public Enemy shall be put to death by the severing of his head from his body."

The Queen had written a heartbreaking request to Parliament on the 6th of January pleading with them to let her see Charles. Her letters were not even opened.

It took two weeks for the news to cross the channel, and when Henrietta-Maria heard it, she refused to believe it. Her life long friend Mdme de Motteville reported that the Queen believed he had been rescued by a mob of outraged Londoners.

She was told of his death by Henry Jermyn, she took the news in silence,so deeply shocked that she stood stock still,
"Motionless as a statue without words. Without tears."

Nothing anyone could say or do moved her. She stood the whole afternoon, and it was only when her sister in law and close friend, the Duchesse of Vendome came to kiss her hand and wept in front of her that she herself started to cry. Henrietta Maria never recovered from the shock of the execution of her husband Charles and she wore mourning clothes for the rest of her life.

After a recovery period in a Carmelite nunnery, Henrietta-Maria returned to advise her son Charles to help him regain the throne.

After Charles II was Restored in 1660, Henrietta Maria returned to England at the invitation of her son, the new King, and being the woman she was, she tried to prevent her son the Duke of York from creating a Royal scandal by marrying the commoner Anne Hyde.

Henrietta was unsuccessful, but as we all know there is a current commoner, The Duchess of Cambridge who is married to a future King, and she seems lovely, so sometimes life works out for the best.

Henrietta lived at Somerset House in London until 1665 when she decided, as she was in failing health, to return to France. She lived in Colombes, near Paris and this is where she died on 21 August 1669. The She Majesty Generalissima was buried in the Cathedral of St Denis.

Charles I, Henrietta-Maria's much loved husband (v)

Elizabeth Cromwell

Elizabeth Cromwell née Bourchier (1598-1665)(vi)

Thunder in the Air

Omen's from Thunder,
Sunday's thunder portends the death of learned men,
judges and others,
Mondays the death of women, Tuesdays plenty of grain,
Wednesdays the death of Harlots and other bloodshed,
Thursdays plenty of sheep and corn,
Fridays the slaughter of a great man and horrible murders,
Saturdays, a general pestilent plague and great death.
Leonard Digges 1556

It was a hot thundery August, harvest time, and Elizabeth Cromwell was 42 or thereabouts when Oliver came through the doors of their farmhouse to tell her that war had been declared on the King. By that time she had borne her husband nine children during their marriage, eight of whom had grown to maturity. Little did she know that her own husband's actions would rob her of her eldest son Oliver. He would die of typhoid at the age of 22 when on campaign as a Parliamentarian officer, and make her second eldest son Richard, humiliated through history as Tumbledown Dick.

Women were working in their kitchens making tansy water to relieve the aching and smelly feet of the harvesters, brewing small beer and making bread. Elizabeth was no different; she was a good cook and made a recipe book that is still in existence today in the Cromwell museum at Ely.

She was the daughter of Frances Crane and Sir James Bouchier of Felstead in Essex. Born into a wealthy merchant class that brought her husband Oliver into contact with the prosperous merchants of London. Oliver was not a Puritan when he married Elizabeth, but saw that becoming one would give him opportunities. It was this connection that allowed him to call on the support of the influential Puritan gentry during the war.

Elizabeth was not a beauty, but a plain woman with a defect in her eye, Samuel Cooper's portraits of her do not show this, and he very carefully describes her as "neither uncomely or undignified in person."

The fact that there is so little known about Elizabeth leads us to believe that by some accounts she was an unremarkable woman. It was said she was thrifty and a good cook and she mainly managed to stay in the background of the tumult that surrounded her husband. She was quiet and loving and let Oliver get on with his work and they exchanged love letters when he was on campaign. Although to read one of the best known letters to her, written in 1650 after the Civil War, there is very little love shown to Elizabeth in it, Oliver starts by saying that he really doesn't have time to write, complains of aches and pains, and seems to be saying that despite what she says in her letters telling him off, he hasn't forgotten her or her children. Note that; - her children.

He says that she is dearer to him than any other creature and that should be enough. He then goes on to mention his messengers who will tell her what has been going on, then sends love to his friends.

Hardly the stuff to get your heart pounding, but after all the years of marriage and stress of having her husband away fighting or ruling the Protectorate, perhaps it was enough for Elizabeth to know she was still secure in her husband's affections.

She must have known of Oliver's liking for intelligent and pretty young women, it was thought he had at least two mistresses during his lifetime, one was the Royalist spy Elizabeth Countess Dysart, and it is said she bore him a child. Elizabeth Cromwell certainly knew her because it was Countess Dysart who asked Elizabeth to use her womanly ways in the bedroom to persuade Oliver to bring back Charles II.

Perhaps she decided that it was best to keep her place. There is a five-year gap in her child-bearing - James born and died in 1632 - to the birth of Mary in 1637. This was during this time that Oliver was MP for Huntingdon.

Perhaps he was away a lot, or stress played a part, or perhaps like many married couples they grew apart, he busy in his political life and she bringing up the children and running the farm.

Unfortunately for Elizabeth when the war started her ordinary life as housewife and mother was blown apart. Although she tried to keep away from politics, she was accused of influencing her husband by Col. Lilburne. He said she was

"steering the helm as well as turning the spit."

Sadly this quiet housewife paid the price for her husband's actions. Elizabeth found she was being made fun of and insulted by being called "Joan" by the Cavaliers, (a name used for a common or rough woman) and they accused her of drunkenness, and adultery. Probably nothing was further from the truth.

But according to the Cavaliers she skulked about the house like a kitchen maid come good, and was ashamed of her sudden rise to fame as if it had been through the lust of her master that she had gained her position.

No doubt she was uncomfortable moving from her quiet country house in Ely to live in the Cockpit in London. But at least she was with her husband. For a provincial housewife from the Fens whose life revolved around the family, preparing the season's provinder, looking after the servants and livestock, London life must have come as a bit of a shock.

The streets smelt of human and animal waste waiting to be collected to be put on the fields around London to fertilise the crops. It was said that if you had eaten vegetables grown from fields around London it took a while to get the rid of the taste!

All the businesses of the time had their own fragrances, the bakers probably being the best, but there were also fishmongers, tanners probably the worst, and barrel-makers, and butchers. The smell of the Thames on a hot summer's day must have caught in the throat, alongside the smoke of burning wood used for cooking and cleaning. Elizabeth must have longed for the clean country air around her home, but threw herself into London and life with her husband.

When she moved to the Cockpit it was one of the unhappiest times of her life. London life was difficult for her, but she took on the running of the household as she was expected to do while the Palace of Whitehall was being prepared for them.

Elizabeth Cromwell had been introduced to Charles I when he was imprisoned at Hampton Court. It seemed to been an odd afternoon outing with her daughter Elizabeth who was the wife of Cromwell's officer Henry Ireton, and her friend the wife of Edward Whalley, where they were afterwards entertained to a meal by the King's gaoler, Mr Ashburnum. It must have been a very strange "ladies who lunch" moment.

Cromwell however saw Elizabeth as no more than his wife. She was there to see to his comforts and his needs she did not, when he came to power, share that with him. Both he and Elizabeth believed that her life was to be domestic and nothing else.

Perhaps she was not a strong-minded woman, and perhaps her son Richard, re-named by the Cavaliers as "Tumbledown Dick", may have shared those traits with her. Richard frequently ran away and changed his name, he had Royalist friends, and Oliver lamented over his lack application to his education, giving him advice on what books he should read to improve himself.

After his father Oliver died, Richard was named as Lord Protector. But the poorly prepared Tumbledown Dick resigned after being held under house arrest. Preferring not to take his father's place, but going home to his farm and marrying and raising his children and his crops with his wife. He died aged 85 fading out from history.

Cromwell was not a man to be knowingly influenced by women, to him Elizabeth was without any ambition, other than to be his wife and mother to his children.

Despite the spin generated by the Cavaliers, he thought that he was not a man to be pushed into doing anything by his wife or any women for that matter. Which made his encounter with Lady Jane Ingleby, whose story will come later in this book, all the more difficult for him to bear.

There are however, a couple of moments in Elizabeth's life that stand out. Strangely, firstly, it is known that she employed six daughters of clergymen to do needlework for her in her own apartments. After the war over a third of English young men were dead, it could have been Elizabeth's way of protecting these young single women by giving them a way to earn a living when there were few young men to marry and keep them.

The other moment was when she asked Oliver to recall Charles II back to the throne. Persuaded by Countess Dysart, whose own application to him must have failed. It would have been an interesting conversation.

As for recalling Charles, she was probably persuaded easily, perhaps to save her son Richard for having to fill his fathers boots. Also it may have gone some way to helping Cromwell regain some forgiveness for the regicide and may have helped improve his popularity.

Elizabeth must have been scared of reprisals if Oliver died, and she knew her son Richard was not the man for the job. He had never fought in the war that killed one of his brothers.

Although he became the MP for Huntingdon and Cambridge he was not interested in politics or history, and Cromwell himself despaired over the boy's behaviour, which was more Cavalier than Roundhead.

Life under the Protectorate was harsh, no dancing, no theatres, no Christmas.

Two women who had been to church twice on the same Sunday were pilloried for going for a walk and chatting as it was thought they were enjoying themselves on the Lord's Day.

When Oliver died in 1658 and after Tumbledown Dick's abortive attempt to take his father's place, in 1660 Elizabeth tried to take some of the Kings possessions with her when she left Whitehall, possibly she thought that they belonged to her now that she was a widow. It's my opinion that she may have tried to take some of the goods to secure a future for herself. She had them hidden in a fruiterer's warehouse in Thames Street in London, but the King's jewels were discovered and returned to Whitehall.

So scared was she of the new Reign of Charles II that at one time she even faked her own death to escape reprisals. She went to Wales to live while the excitement of the Restoration was at its peak.

Elizabeth wrote to Charles II pleading to be allowed to go to the country and live a quiet life.
However the Cavaliers were as "cavalier" in their forgiveness of the former Protectress Joan as they were about everything else, except the Regicides.

She was given a pension and allowed to live out her last days in the house of her daughter Elizabeth and son in law John Claypole at Norborough in Northamptonshire. She is buried in Norbough Church.

Her legacy and influence on her children meant that her surviving sons and daughters married into the aristocracy and one of her sons entertained Charles II to dine with him.

Although Oliver was not so lucky, already dead, his body was exhumed and his head cut off and put on a pike. It was Charles II's revenge for the death of his much loved father.

The Ashmolean Museum now has Cromwell's death mask. As for Elizabeth there are few portraits of her, even the Cromwell Museum in Ely has only a portrait of Cromwell's mother Elizabeth, but not of the woman who stood in the shadow of her husband, who bore him his "two families" who pleaded to try and get him to save himself and took the abuse thrown at her in his name.

In the Cromwell Museum in Ely is her recipe book with the recipe for Eel Pie being the most prevalent. Living in a county where eels were abundant, she made good use of them. But her husband had more exotic tastes with his favourite meal being calves livers with oranges.

*Oliver was not born a Cromwell, but changed his name as he admired Henry VIII's advisor Thomas Cromwell.

Jane Whorwood
Royalist Spy

Red headed Jane was born in London into the world of the Scottish Royalist court in 1612. Her father, William Ryder, worked in the royal stables for King James and her mother, Elizabeth, was laundress for the Queen, Anne of Denmark. When Jane was five her father died and a couple of years later her mother re-married a more important courtier, another Scot, called James Maxwell who was then a groom of the bedchamber.

Jane was nineteen when she married the fifteen year old hot-headed Brome Whorwood. He was heir to the Manor of Headington in Oxford and Sandwell in Staffordshire. A year later in 1635 Jane gave birth to their first child, Brome Whorwood, named for his father. Two more children followed in quick succession, Elizabeth, 1638 who lived only two years, and Diana 1639. One or both children were probably born at Sandwell.

At the start of the Civil War, Brome disappeared abroad to Europe and remained there until 1645, leaving Jane with their two surviving children. Jane moved her young family to another of the Brome's properties, Holton House, on the outskirts of Oxford near to where the Royal court had been moved.

It was here that Jane was to start her adventures as a Royal Spy. Jane was striking looking, tall, red haired and her face was marked by the pox. Not the sort of woman who you would have thought would be inconspicuous moving gold for the King or acting as his secret agent.

Anthony Wood, A Parliament spy reported in April 1648 that:

> *"Mistress Whorwood is a tall, well-fashioned and well-languaged gentlewoman, with a round visage and with pock holes in her face, red haired, as her son Brome was, exceedingly loyal, understanding and of good judgement, the*

most loyal to King Charles in his miseries of any woman in England."

Jane was able to use her mother and step-father's positions in the Royal Court and their connections to help her in her new found career. Maxwell, her step-father, became a private financier to Charles I in 1629, and it was his merchant contacts who helped Jane smuggle funds for the King during the Civil War.

Jane found that even her mother's job as a laundress had it's uses. She managed to organise nearly 2000lbs of gold that Sir Paul Pindar donated in London, to be delivered to Oxford, hidden in barrels of soap. The gold was to be used to send Henrietta-Maria and Charles II to France and safety.

Jane worked tirelessly throughout the Civil War, and once again the King was relying on the guile of women to help him fund his war against Parliament. Jane had contacted Royalists from London to Edinburgh secretly taking information from the King's supporters and relaying it between them, even informing the King himself.

It wasn't long before Parliament caught up with Charles, and Jane was determined to help the King escape from their clutches. She went to see William Lilly, one of the most famous astrologers of the time. Astrology in the 17th Century was a science and the domain of men, where today men dismiss it, and it is women who see the value in it.

William Lilley told Jane that the King should head into Essex to hide, but the King decided to take matters into his own hands. He used the excuse that the marching up and down of the Guards outside his rooms in Hampton Court was keeping his fragile daughter Elizabeth awake, and he ran away out of a back door as soon as they were removed.

Unfortunately, Charles believed he had a friend in the Governor of Carisbrooke Castle, Colonel Hammond. As usual he was wrong, he had escaped from one prison to walk straight into another.

Again he tried to escape, late at night a couple of his cavaliers had brought a horse for him, all he had to do was to squeeze through the bars of his window and lower himself onto the horse. The story goes that he could not get through the bars with his doublet on and refused to leave it behind, so the escape was foiled. If it was me I'd have taken the doublet off, thrown it to my rescuers and squeezed through the bars, but then I'm a woman and can think of the logic of this sort of thing!

Jane had heard of this escape attempt and it was once again a consultation with William Lilly who helped her formulate another plan. Now this is where history and legend merge. It is said that Lilly gave Jane a file which she then baked into a cake. When the King received it he did not know what it was having never seen one before, so didn't use it to file the bars of his window to escape. So the famous file in a cake joke was born.

Jane waited for several weeks aboard a ship she had helped to obtain with the aim of sailing him to safety in Holland.

Not one for giving up on a task, Jane again visited Charles in Carisbrooke Castle, to make plans for another escape attempt. They wrote to each other frequently, it was widely assumed that Jane and Charles became lovers in July of 1648. Although this is not conclusively proved, it is strange that she was never mentioned in Charles' letters to Henrietta-Maria. Fragments of their correspondence that have been found use lewd words, but perhaps this was all part of the deception to allow Jane to enter his chambers. They wrote to each other using ciphers and she sometimes signed herself JW or Hellen.

Charles obviously valued Jane's assistance because he wrote to his trusted ally William Hopkins:

> *"You may freely trust Whorwood in anything that concerns my service, for I have had perfect trial of her friendship to me. I cannot be more confident of any."*

On the 30th of January 1646, the King was to walk to his execution in Whitehall. As it was very cold he dressed in two shirts so that he would not shiver on his way to the scaffold and his enemies would think he was afraid. Earlier that morning he had been saying a tearful goodbye to his two remaining children. Elizabeth cried so sorrowfully that her tears even softened the most hard hearted of the enemies around them.

When Charles walked to his death through the crowds at the Banqueting House on that cold January morning, a tall, handsome, red haired woman pushed through the crowd towards him. Lady Jane Whorwood took his hand, and kissed Charles in greeting, confirming to many that they were indeed lovers. For this blatant and brave show of affection to a friendless man about to die, Jane was to pay.

She was imprisoned in 1651 and fined for defrauding Parliament and funding Royalists. Worse was to come.

Later that year she was sent home to her husband Brome. He had taken up with one of their servants, Katherine Allen, who was living as his wife. Jane was locked up in the tower of Holton House, frequently beaten and verbally abused.

It is my opinion, and mine only, that Brome was jealous of Jane, of her closeness to the King, of her single-minded bravery and endurance when he had virtually ran away and left her to it at the beginning of the war. The Whorwood family had described Brome as always being a bit of a hothead. But to me he was a bully, a wife beater and a coward.

Jane must have been terrified. Her life had changed from that of a person who had been so brave, clever, and loved, she was used to going out and doing what she wanted by herself. She had been in charge of her own and the King's life, she now found herself a prisoner in her own home who could not fight back. At times Brome beat her so badly that she was seriously injured.

In 1657 her son, Brome the younger, died when his ship sunk on a pleasure trip with friends to the Isle of Wight. This must have triggered something in Jane because she managed to escape from Holton House, always fearing that her husband would come after her to kill her.

Like Hester Tradescant, Jane Whorwood was to become involved in long legal battles that lasted the whole of her life until she died. Brome fought her for the small amount of money she was entitled to. Even when Jane had the locals of Holton stand up for her, saying they'd witnessed the terrible abuse she had suffered, she received nothing.

She was never recognised for her service to the King and the Royalist cause during the Civil War and she died in poverty in April 1684 aged 72.
This was not how I wanted her story to end, I wished she could have had a better life after all her adventures, some of which were funny and some sad.

I would have loved to have seen the King's face when the file was found in the cake! Did he think someone had left a cooking implement in by accident or did he think he was lucky not to have broken a tooth on it?

I think of her pushing her way through a crowd of jeering Londoners, tall and striking. Her red hair dressed under a felt hat with her poor pock marked face painted and powdered. She edged towards Charles to show him that there was one person who cared and was brave enough to show it by grabbing his hand and kissing his cheek.

There are no portraits that I could find of Jane. There is one of her sister, but with a different father there may not be much of a likeness between them.

When Jane was in London she had gone to see William Lilley the astrologer again on the Kings' business and he refused her entry because there was plague in the house.

"It's not the plague I'm afraid of Sir, but the Pox."

she joked pushing past him.

She is buried in Holton church in Oxford.

Lady Anne Halkett

(née Murray)

Anne Murray was the daughter of Charles I's teacher Thomas, her mother Jane, was the governess to the King and Queen's growing family. Anne was the youngest of the family born in 1622. She was given a good education by her parents, and when her father died, her mother continued to teach Jane. She could speak French, dance, sew, knew enough medicine and surgery to became a midwife later in her life. She was also very religious, she prayed every day and regularly attended church.

Does all this sound too good to be true? Well yes it was, Anne Murray had one weakness: Men. She fell in love frequently and too hard. When she was twenty one she fell in love with Thomas Howard or Lord Howard of Escrick as he was formally known.

Thomas was expected to marry for money, Howards were a distinguished family, but poor. The clever daughter of a couple of teachers was not the match his family were looking for.

Jane, Anne's mother, decided to take things into her own hands. She did not want her daughter to marry an impoverished young Lord and live in hardship for the rest of her life. So she had Anne share a room probably with a maid, so that Thomas could not visit her and forbade her to see him again.

So Anne said goodbye to her first love wearing a blindfold, so that she could keep her promise to her mother not to see him again. Unsurprisingly Anne hardly spoke to her mother for nearly a year and two months. She swore never to marry unless Thomas did. Thomas vowed he would never marry, but financial and family pressures make him break his vow, and he married in 1646. His marriage was known to be unhappy.

When her mother Jane died in 1647, Anne went to live with her brother and his wife. It was while she was living there she met the dashing Irish Cavalier and Royalist agent Colonel Joseph Bamfield. He was a handsome charming man by all accounts calling on her many times at her brother's London house. He was also married.

Although she knew this, Anne embarked on a passionate affair with the James Bond of the day, and it wasn't long before he was asking for her help.

He had been tasked to arrange the young James, Duke of York's escape from the Tower of London and his Parliament captors. Colonel Bamfield had managed, through a contact, to arrange a visit to the Duke of York. It was possibly Anne's idea to disguise the young Duke as a girl, she told Joseph to take a ribbon with him to measure James' waist and the length of a skirt.

Dressed as a young gentlewoman James, the 15 year old, Duke of York could pass through London to Gravesend and hopefully board a ship to Holland.

Anne gave the measurements to her tailor, who was a bit puzzled at making a dress for a young woman of such a strange size "and bignesse". He said he'd made many gowns and suits, but had never met a person like this in his life. She thought that her tailor must have worked out what was going on, if he did, he said nothing, producing a light and dark coloured mohair overdress with a scarlet underskirt for the Duke's disguise.

On the 20th of April James was playing hide and seek with his brother and sister, he often did this, he was good at it and it sometimes took them both an hour to find him. On this day James told the gardener he was at his "usuall sport", borrowed a key to the gate and ran down the toilet stairs to where Colonel Bamfield was waiting.

Anne was in a rented house by the river, the Colonel told her and his servant to wait until ten o'clock. If they hadn't arrived by then something must have happened and she would have to look after herself. Ten o'clock came and went and Col. Bamfield's servant was getting worried, wanting to

leave, but Anne said she had come to help His Highness and was not leaving until she'd done what she'd come to do.
There was a clatter on the stairs and Anne had her heart in her mouth expecting to see soldiers burst through the door, but it was Colonel Bamford and the young Duke shouting "Quickly, quickly, dress me."

The girl's clothes fitted really well, and Anne thought he looked very pretty in them! She had found out what his favourite cake was and gave him that and some food for his journey, growing boys are always hungry. Then the Colonel led his new young lady friend to the barge to take them to Gravesend and onto a ship to Holland.

Anne hurried back to her brothers house. Nothing seemed out of the ordinary as she made her way back with her maid. Once it had been realised what had happened on following day, there was a call for all the ports to be closed, but the royal horse had safely bolted.

The Colonel came back to London and for a few months Anne was his willing errand girl. "Being the only person I can trust." Coming and going from his lodgings could have given Anne a bad reputation, but she didn't care, she was serving the Royalist cause, and that was what mattered.
One day on a visit to see the Colonel he told her that he had heard his wife had died. He didn't seem unduly upset, but he told Jane that he wanted to keep it quiet, so that his wife's money and house would not be sequestered by Parliament. Shortly afterwards he proposed to Anne and she accepted on the condition that they married when the King's affairs were more prosperous.

Anne moved in with the Colonel and lived with him for two years, unaware that his wife was still alive, and that he'd lied to her.

Later in her life Anne practised medicine in Scotland, and followed in her mother's footsteps becoming a governess to the two daughters of a widower Sir James Halkett. She married him in 1656 they were happily married for 20 years, but she found that when he died, she was left with hardly any money to support the family. She again had to make her living as her parents did by teaching the children of nobility.

Her financial difficulties eased when James II provided her with a pension for her services to him during the English Civil War, one of the very few women to be rewarded for her service to the Royalist cause.

Anne was a writer, and when she died, she left behind 21 folio and quarto manuscript volumes written between 1644 and the late 1690s.
She was one of the first women to write her autobiography in 1677. She wrote about what she read, her dreams, and her hopes for her children. Her Memoirs are personal and political comments on events during the English Civil War. Probably written between 1677 and 1678. She talks in detail about the men in her life and marriage. She has tried to put her emotions and those of her lovers into her life story, and as in her life, constantly mentions the murder of her beloved King.

There is a waxwork figure of her in her old age, writing her memoirs, in Abbot house, Dunfermline.

Elizabeth Dysart

Elizabeth of the Sealed Knot (vii)

Elizabeth Murray, Countess of Dysart was born in 1626, the daughter of Charles 1st 's whipping boy William Dysart and his wife Catherine Bruce.

A whipping boy was a boy of the same age as the young King, educated alongside him, who would take the punishment for the him if the King had done anything wrong. William and Charles became firm friends, and when Charles became King, he granted William the lease on Ham house when he rose to be a Gentleman of the Bedchamber.

Elizabeth was the eldest of five daughters, small in stature, like her father and red-haired. Anyone who had red hair was thought to have magical qualities, and perhaps even a witch. Her father gave the same education to Elizabeth as he would have done to a son, almost unheard of at the time. It was to acquit her well as she moved through the political morass of the day.

Amazing to think than even today, less than one fifth of the people living in Great Britain have natural red hair, the Celtic curse. Even in a world where different ethnicities, the disabled and people with alternative sexualities have been widely accepted, redheads alone are still singled out as targets for prejudice.

As in the 17century, and today, the minority of red-haired people are amongst the most famous in the world. I bet you can name five without any trouble at all.

Back to Elizabeth, it is she that we have to thank for the Sealed Knot which was a secret society she helped form so that she could support the new King Charles II during his exile and the start of the second Civil War, for Elizabeth was yet another female spy.

Elizabeth probably first met The Puritan Lord General, Oliver Cromwell at her home, Ham House in 1647. Her mother, a very astute woman, invited him to try and keep the sequestering Commissioners away, and keep Ham in the family for a little longer.

Cromwell had a weakness for clever pretty young women, and Elizabeth was exactly that. She helped her mother entertain the Lord General, forced to be happy and interested in his company and hide her Royalist allegiances.

When she was twenty two her father found her a suitable husband and in 1648 she married Sir Lionel Tollemache. He was of good reputation, good family and good inheritance. Probably more important to William, he was completely uninterested in politics, but he was devoted to Elizabeth.

She seemed to be constantly pregnant, having given birth to eleven children during their marriage. One of the five surviving to adulthood was Thomas Tollemache, who was believed to be Oliver Cromwell's son.

When her mother died in August 1649, Elizabeth with the help of her husband Lionel, took over the care of her three younger sisters and her cousin. Her mother Catherine had managed to save Ham House from being seized by Parliament before she died. She did it so effectively that a second attempt to sequester the house after she died, failed.

After the Battle of Worcester in 1651 Cromwell decided to go to Hampton Court to rest and regroup. The battle had exhausted him and he found himself Elizabeth's neighbour. Lady Tollmache made him very welcome, having been brought up by her mother to ingratiate herself with those in power. Thomas Tollmache was born in 1651 so it is quite possible despite his joking claims to the contrary, that he was not actually Cromwell's son.

In fact his mother was disgusted by her liaison with Cromwell. She said after his death - roughly translated from the Early Modern English:

> *" There are some in this assembly divers that I know to be very considerable and some to whom I am obliged, but certainly had the old one (Cromwell) lived, there was none that could say so much or expect the least reality. I can only say I did know him* and hope I shall never know his like again."*

(*in the biblical sense, i.e.sex)
What Elizabeth did do was to use her influence on Cromwell as much as she could. She saved the life of another Royalist spy from the scaffold, Lord Lauderdale in 1651. He was so grateful he left her fifteen hundred pounds in gold in his will.

Unfortunately, she could not save the life of Charles Ist. She even tried to get Cromwell's wife, another Elizabeth, to petition the Lord Protector by using her wifely skills in the bedroom to ask Oliver to proclaim Charles as King and keep Cromwell as his first Minister, so keeping the Lord Protectorate he had fought so hard for.

Elizabeth Cromwell was a frightened woman, she was worried that Oliver would be assassinated, or if there was a Royalist coup, her family would be executed, so she agreed to try out the plan.

I think Elizabeth Cromwell's skills were more culinary than sexual, so it didn't work. Oliver, like so many men long married, no longer listened to his wife.

In 1653 The Sealed Knot was born as a secret Royalist organisation. William Murray visited his daughter and told her that there was going to be a Royalist resistance movement. Elizabeth immediately got involved, able to use her close association with Cromwell to her advantage, she corresponded with exiled Royalists and even visited Charles II.

The Sealed Knot's main leaders at the time were Lord Belasyse, Lord Loughborough, Sir Richard Willys, Sir William Compton, who was their intelligence officer, Colonel John Russell and Colonel Edward Villiers.

Elizabeth must have been a very strong woman with lots of stamina, she was constantly pregnant, and told her friend Dorothy Osborne when she fell ill with smallpox,

> *"When she saw that she had the pox coming out on her, she said it was not a convenient time to have the pox, she had business to see to, and she was NOT going to be sick."*

After his wife's death in 1649 her father William had left England to live with Charles II in Holland, returning to England shortly before his own death in 1655. When William died Elizabeth inherited his title and became Countess Dysart.

Elizabeth used Cromwell's weakness for her, although he thought he was using her weakness for him. After all she moved in Royalist circles, often he tried to gain information from her, she became one of his "Favourites". He visited her often and wrote to her, although none of his "love" letters have been found.

Elizabeth on the other hand kept Ham House, her possessions, her husband and her family intact, it was a price not many women would be prepared to pay. Gossip from the starving and jealous Royalists abroad abounded, they called her a witch because of her red hair and the way they thought she could influence events.

Years later Elizabeth admitted that she was a "knowing" woman, she had the power of prediction, and good intuition. She had used this to good effect during her time as a spy and message carrier.

In 1669 after the Restoration of the Monarchy, Lionel, her quiet, loving, supporting - yet probably much cuckolded husband, died in France.

At the age of 43 Elizabeth found herself widowed. With almost indecent haste she became the Mistress of John Maitland, 1st Duke of Lauderdale, the Royalist spy she had saved from execution. On his wife's death in 1672 the couple immediately married.

Oliver Cromwell - Elizabeth's "Old one." (viii)

John was made Baron Petersham by his friend King Charles II and the couple led a privileged and wealthy lifestyle at the Court until John's death in 1682. Then as with many women of the time Elizabeth was embroiled in a legal dispute with her brother-in-law over her late husbands' financial affairs. Elizabeth Maitland died, at the age of 72, on 5 June 1698 at Ham House the home she loved. She is buried with other members of the Dysart family in a vault under the chancel of Petersham Parish Church.

Hester Tradescant and the Ark

Hester Tradescant and her children (ix)

Hester Tradescant was born Hester Pooke, around 1608. This is a photo I took of her portrait in the Ashmolean Museum in Oxford. Hester looks frightened and miserable after being deserted by her husband John Tradescant the Younger in the middle of the English Civil War.

Hester's cousin was Thomas de Critz he was the court painter, he painted the portrait above, called Hester and her Children. She is well dressed and on her left hand is a small garnet wedding ring.

However, the children she so tenderly touches in the portrait are not her own, they are the son and daughter of her husband John Tradescant the Younger, and his first wife Jane Hurte.

John was King Charles I and Queen Henrietta Maria's gardener. He worked with his elderly father, also called John Tradescant, in the gardens of the

Royal Palaces of Oatlands (now demolished), and Hatfield. The older John Tradescant had led an exciting life of travel collecting rarities from Holland and France to add to the Royal Collections and to his own curiosities cabinet.

John Tradescant the Younger and his first wife Jane were a true love match, a rarity when most marriages were contracted for the benefit of both couples' families. Jane's family were cloth and linen traders in London whom she visited often and it is thought that on one of these visits to London she contracted the plague. Sadly her baby son John was so young at the time that he grew up without ever knowing his mother.

There is a beautiful portrait of Jane Hurte in the Ashmolean Museum in Oxford. I hope baby John got to know his mother a little by seeing her smiling face looking out at him, dressed in her finery, looking a confident happy woman.

Her husband John the Younger, found her death in June 1635 very hard to bear. He paid the exceptional sum of £100 to have her buried in the family vault in Lambeth. He could not bear the thought of his beloved wife being stripped and thrown into a plague pit.

John the Younger left his two young children in the care of his father and their servants in 1637 when he was sent to his lands in Virginia by King Charles to collect various rarities of plants, flowers and shells.

A year later while he was still away, his father fell ill. John Tradescant the Elder died in the April of 1638 when he was 68 years old. John the Younger made his way back to his home in Lambeth as quickly as he could to his two children, Frances and John.

John must have met Hester at one of the Palaces where he worked while she mixed paints for her relative, the portrait painter Thomas de Critz.

Hester was a plain 25-year-old spinster working for a living, and John was a widower with a business to run and two young children. They were both part of the new “middling sort”. Up and coming artisans, craftsmen and traders making their way in life in the towns and cities.

Strangely both were Puritans who worked for the King and Queen, both struggling on their own, it must have seemed common sense to both of them to contract a marriage.

In retrospect it was perhaps the worst decision Hester ever made.

They married on the 1st October 1638. There was no time for a courtship. It was a business arrangement, although by the law at the time, all marriages had to be consummated.

Hester had to give her body to a man that she had only known for a few months. It must have been difficult for her to submit to man she knew only wanted a housekeeper and a stepmother for his children.

At that time it was the custom for family and friends to wait outside the bedroom door cheering, jeering and celebrating, waiting to hear that the job was done. Poor Hester.

As time went on Hester and John had no children of their own. Probably because John was away for most of their marriage, or it may have been that once the marriage was legal, there was no need for them to sleep together. Hester had traded her lonely single life, for a lonely married one.

The Tradescant family were in a difficult position when the English Civil War broke out, by nature Puritans, but working for the Royal family at their palaces. It would not be long before John would have been called to fight for the King or Parliament and it was a call he did not want to answer.

In October 1642 after the battle of Edgehill, John decided to go back to his lands in Virginia feeling confident enough in Hester's abilities to look after his interests at home.

It was a difficult time for a woman on her own, in the middle of a raging Civil War, looking after two children who were not hers. Hester came to love and protect the four-year-old John and the nine-year-old Frances when they came into her care. Young John had known no other mother, they became close.

Hester was a very busy woman, she was running their orchard, plant nursery business and the Ark. Which was their own collection of curiosities, that made up the Tradescant Museum started by John Tradescant the Elder.

Tradescant's House, South Lambeth (from Tennant), wood engraving, ca. 1883. (x)

Hester had a lot on her mind, it wasn't long before Frances was rising sixteen and it would be soon time to look for a husband for her. Without John, Hester felt she had to get Frances somewhere safe. There was always the possibility of raids on the house, she had heard of soldiers invading private households and she knew what would happen to a pretty blonde sixteen year old girl.

Frances' great uncle Alexander Norman, a cooper, lived and worked at the Tower of London, Hester reasoned that there could be no safer place in London. So a marriage was arranged between Frances and her great uncle.

Alexander Norman was described as being about fifty six at the time they tied the knot in January 1645. They married at the city church of St Bartholomew the Less, where Frances' age was given as “about nineteen.” As Hester gave Frances' age it may have been an exaggeration.

Little is known of Frances after she left the family home in Lambeth, it is known they had no offspring and that her husband Alexander Norman had died before the death of her father, John the Younger, in 1662, leaving Frances recorded as being a widow.

Perhaps Frances at the age of thirty something married again and moved to the country with her new husband as there is no trace of her in London records.

John returned from Virginia in 1650 to live at Lambeth near to St Mary's Churchyard, (it is now the Museum of Garden History), but in the 1650s it was far enough out of London to get away from the plague. Hester decided to open the house to paying guests, who were people trying to get away from the war, or the plague or sometimes husbands and wives. It was company for her and extra income as the payments from the King and Queen had ceased, the Civil War had no time for ornate gardens.

It was in June 1650 that the thirty three year old Royalist Officer Elias Ashmole came to stay with the Tradescants. He had been approaching several rich widows older than himself, with a view to making a good marriage and brought his new wife, twenty years his senior, Mary Lady Mainwaring to visit the curiosities at Lambeth.

Elias had quickly befriended John with a common interest in the Tradescant collection and offered to catalogue the collection for him. Hester looked on him as a family friend who shared the same interests as her husband and welcomed him into her home.

Life was turbulent and to quote a current popular song of the time "The World Turned Upside Down."

1652 turned out to be a bad year for the Tradescants. Hester's stepson John Tradescant the third must had become a worry to her. When his father left for Virginia to avoid the war his young son John decided to run away to join the Royalist army as a drummer. On his return aged 19 John committed suicide in the orchard at Lambeth unable to live under Cromwell's Protectorate.

Hester was heartbroken, as was her husband. They buried him in the family tomb four days later with his mother and grandfather. In a time when death from illness and disease was all too common, no-one expected a young person to die in this way. Despite her best efforts she must have felt she had let her husband and stepson down.

Unfortunately for the trusting couple their new friend Elias Ashmole was ambitious and untrustworthy, having married Lady Mainwaring who, in his own words, "gave me the best elixir I enjoyed, money, lands, jointures, wherewith I purchased books, rarities and other things".

He liked to use the law and it wasn't long before the crafty Elias had started to take out lawsuits against his wife's family and even his wife herself. It was a dark shadow of things to come for Hester.

One evening John had gone to the Tavern to drink with Ashmole and four strangers. Later he was carried back to his house much the worse for wear, he was thrown into his chair clutching a piece of parchment. Hester pulled it out of his hand to find he had signed his whole collection of curiosities over to Ashmole whilst in his cups.

Ashmole gave her a shilling and asked her to sign the deed, confused and not quite knowing what was going on she did as she was asked. Only later did she realise what she'd done. Seventeenth century women had it ground into them to do as they were told. Most did so without question.

After reading the deed she shouted at John - this translated from Early Modern English-

> *"What have you done? How could you have been so stupid to let them do this to you?" She threw the paper at him. "They've embezzled you, they can take everything we've worked for, and easily."*

The next morning when John had sobered up they re-read the deed. They took off the wax seal, destroyed it and scratched out his name. John wanted to burn the parchment, but Hester told him to keep it to show people what sort of man Elias Ashmole really was, and how badly he had treated his friend. John swore Ashmole would not get a penny of his.

Hester was a strong woman, she had to be, and hadn't fallen for Ashmole's hyperbole, but even a strong woman had very little say in the seventeenth century.

A sense of relief followed as the Tradescants thought that they had brought their life back to normal, with John amending his will to leave everything to his wife, and after her demise to either Oxford or Cambridge colleges - whatever she thought fit.

What they didn't know, was that Ashmole was a lawyer and had seen to it that his document was binding. All he had to do now was wait. He used his time to ingratiate himself with the restored King Charles II and climb the greasy pole of royal favour becoming Windsor Herald just two weeks after Charles II returned to the Throne.

Life in Lambeth continued much as usual, with the curiosities being shown to everyone - even women - for the price of a shilling. John was fifty now and no longer ambitious. However as life sometimes does, it threw the Tradescants a curve ball.

The Master of the Revels claimed by showing their rarities they were putting on a performance. Thereby in contempt of the Master of the Revels and were called to account for themselves.

John complained to the King who upheld his complaint and the case was dropped. It was supposed that Elias Ashmole had advised the King to do this, after all in the long run, it would be of benefit to himself.

Hester however remembered this as a kindness which she repaid Elias during the great fire of London, allowing him to store books, paintings, furniture and valuables at her Lambeth home, which he brought down by barge on the Thames.

Another two years of trials and tribulations followed for the Tradescants, but the stress must have taken it's toll on John's health, even though he thought himself healthy, he died suddenly in 1662 at the age of 53.

Unusually for a woman, Hester took it upon herself to design his tomb. It was such an original design that Samuel Pepys wanted an engraving of it. Carved into the stone were shells, crocodiles, pyramids, a hydra, a skull, trees, a lion and their family crest. Hester had represented the life of the family she had joined in the spectacular fashion in which they had explored the world and collected their curiosities.

Within days of John's death, Ashmole was at Hester's heels with a lawsuit to claim the Rarities he had persuaded John to sign away to him while drunk. Ashmole had gathered together the best lawyers in the land.

But Hester was not without her supporters, a leading churchman Foulke Bignell, a public notary Richard Hoare, her kinsman Cornelius de Neve and her friend, the famous artist, Wenceslas Hollar.

After much legal wrangling where Hester stood her ground which was not an easy thing for a woman to do when opposed by such great men, It was decided that Hester would keep the rarities for her lifetime as specified in John's will. After her death they would then go to Ashmole in part as payment for his cataloguing of the curiosities.

Hester's case was unproven, and she found herself looking after the collection for Ashmole for the duration of her lifetime. She was devastated. She had lost her livelihood. She was also accused of embezzling Ashmole out of the curiosities and treated like a criminal.

Elias Ashmole had won, but he had not finished with Hester yet.

To keep the wolf from the door, Hester sold items collected by her, after her husbands death.

Hester was alone, but by no means friendless. She still had buyers for her curiosities, one of whom was William Courten. He was the grandson of a wealthy London merchant, he continued to buy curiosities from her in the Summer and Autumn of 1667.

Hester kept her gardens and collections open to visitors even posting advertisements that the late Mr Tradescant's curiosities could still be seen.

Note how Hester did not use her own name in the advertisement. However ingenious and creative Hester had become to protect herself, she was not ready for Elias Ashmole's next move. In October 1674 he bought Mrs Blackamore's house next door so that he could see what Hester was up to. The odd visit to show his friends "his rarities" Hester could just about bear, but having him next door where he could come across at any time must have been unbearable for her. At one point he even broke down the dividing garden wall between the houses so that he could climb over and spy on her. To add insult to injury he demanded an inventory of the rarities and served a writ to ensure it happened.

She now had Elias Ashmole watching every her every move. He even claimed he stopped Hester's collection from being robbed.

All of this was too much for Hester, the strain must have been unbearable. She lost her temper and told him in front of her neighbours to take the curiosities- take them all. Take them all now or she'd throw them all out into the street. Ashmole claimed he tried to get her friends and neighbours to intervene. But Hester would not hear of it.

But in his usual way Elias Ashmole harried the ageing Hester with legal documents, forcing her sign in front of witnesses. Telling everyone "Mrs Tradescant was willing to deliver the rarities up to me." Ashmole did take the rarities to his own house next door, in two lots. he first on the 26th November 1674 and the rest on the 1st of December, proudly noting he carried them by himself to his new house at South Lambeth.

Not happy that he had robbed Hester of her living, he then accused her of slandering his name, forcing her to sign a document saying how much she had wronged Elias Ashmole by making false accusations to blemish his good name. She had to have this witnessed by Katherine King and Thomas de Critz both good friends of hers.

In 1678 Hester was found drowned in the pond in her orchard. It was generally believed at the time that she could not bear any more of Ashmole and his lawsuits. However, others think she may have been murdered.

Even after her death Ashmole could not leave the poor woman alone. Wanting the two rings she had left to her two good friends, Sarah de Creets and Katherine King, as was his way, he took them to court to claim them.

For some reason he particularly wanted Hester's garnet wedding ring that she wears in so many of her portraits, claiming it was taken from the rarities. He also laid claim to her "very greate personal estate, consisting of monies, jewels, plate and good household stuffe, bonds, bills and other goodes" as compensation for his having to continually take out litigation against her.

There is a story told, I don't know whether this is true or not, that Hester's friends would not give in to his bullying tactics. In court in the case of the garnet ring, the Judge thumped his gavel, stared at Ashmole, and shouted. "Enough Sir, you have had enough."

By 1686 both Hester's friends had died and only then did Ashmole give up trying to claim the remnants of the Tradescant estate.

Hester rests in the tomb she designed for the family she joined, protected and perhaps came to love.

In another time she could have been a proficient portrait painter. In her time she was artistic, became an astute business woman, a quick learner, a loving mother,and an extremely brave woman. She stood against powerful men in a time when women were dismissed as little more than housekeepers and breeding mares.

The Tradescant tomb in the gardens of the Royal Horticultural Museum designed by Hester (xi)

Lady Anne Cunningham
Defender of Scotland

(xii)

On the 5th of June 1639 when most of the people were working in the fields shearing their sheep, a forty one year old Scottish widow was fighting for what she believed in on the battlefields of Berwick.

Her husband James Hamilton the second Marquess of Hamilton had died at the age of 36 in London whilst attending Parliament. Obviously not a good speaker as his last speech it was said, was not worth dying for. Where his wife Lady Anne was strong and opinionated, with " her masculine spirit", her husband on the other hand was easy going and fey. They were probably a good match complimenting each others strengths and weaknesses.

They had two sons, James and William. James seemed to have inherited his mother's strength of character, although not her goodness or generosity.

History says that he might have had a hand in murdering his own father by poison. If he did, it was because the new Marquess received all his father's titles, and also the same annuity his father had received from the court of £2500 sterling.

It was thought he was probably helped by the hand of his friend, the Duke of Buckingham, George Villiers. Strangely King James was to die in similar circumstances only three weeks later.
It seemed that both young men were now moving up in the Court of Charles I of England.

However, James was no match for his formidable mother Lady Anne. James had thrown his lot in with Charles I against the Scottish Covenanters and took an English fleet of ships filled with troops to Forth in 1639 to overthrow them. He was greeted by the sight of his mother on horseback, holding a pistol in each hand, at the head of a Troop of Horse. She was among thousands waiting on the shoreline of Leith waiting to repel the invaders.

She shouted that she would be the first to shoot him should he try to land and attack the Covenanters. This brave women had the legend grow up around her that she had loaded her pistol with gold balls to shoot her own son. What is certain though is that she did visit him on his ship, giving the waiting thousands hope that "The son of such a mother will do us no harm."

I would have liked to have been a fly on the wall for that conversation, Lady Anne was a staunch defender of the Presbyterian Church in Scotland against Charles I's attempts to convert the whole of Scotland to Anglicanism. She was known for her active leadership in the National Covenantant resistance movement.

The Marquess did not land his troops. Whether he was convinced by his mother not to do so, we do not know. Perhaps she pointed out to him that he did not have enough troops - only about three or four thousand - against the thousands she had lined up on the coast. Or it could have been that he had just heard of the English defeat by the Scots at Kelso with the death of about three hundred men.

Staring from his ship at the lines of shouting troops, his own countrymen, along the coastline must have been daunting for the young Marquess. He decided to retreat.

At Berwick, Lady Anne Cunningham led a troop of mixed sex cavalry into action against the King. They rode under a banner showing a hand repelling a prayer book with the motto - God, the King, Religion and the Covenant. The result led to the Scots' the right to a free church assembly and a free parliament. She died in 1647 aged 67.

In her time she was said to be a masculine woman, today we would call her a strong woman. The remaining portraits of her are badly faded, but if you look at her eyes, you will see she was a woman who knew her own mind and had a steely determination.

Margaret Cavendish Duchess of Newcastle

Margaret Cavendish (xiii)

Mad Madge Newcastle is a woman after my own heart. Whenever she was told that a woman should not or could not do something, she did it, saying her mind was too big to be held down. She wasn't always like that, it took a series of adventures and the love of a good man to give her the confidence to truly be herself.

Born into a Royalist family in 1623, as the youngest of eight, Margaret Lucas was quiet and shy. Her personality began to show as she got older, in the way she adapted her clothes to her own fashion, in the way that she passionately wanted to be a published writer. In her time only a very few books written by women were published, then usually under assumed names or posthumously.

Unheard of, a woman writer. In one of her books, she actually apologises for being a woman, stating:

> *"Condemn me not as a dishonour of your sex, for setting forth this work; for it is harmless and free from all dishonesty; I will not say from vanity for that is so natural to our sex as it were unnatural not to be so"*

She wrote about twenty three books, consisting of stories, poems, plays and the first-ever science-fiction novel, called The Blazing World - still in print today.

She was like her father in that she married for love not money or position. Like her mother in that she was a clever woman, taking over a man's duties despite being in a man's world.

Her young life she describes as blissful, rounds of parties and visits, surrounded by her family and friends, the Summers spent in the country, the Winters in London for the season. Going to Hyde Park, newly opened by the King, to see the rich and famous parading around, showing off in the latest style of coach and horses.
In 1642 she states:

> *"this unnatural war came like a whirlwind,which felled down their houses,where some in the wars were crushed to death."*

Little did she know then that her family, the Lucas', were going to be drawn into the war bringing death and destruction to many of them. She may have even survived the sack of her mother's house in Colchester, having been imprisoned with the other women of her family while the townspeople looted and destroyed their lands and household. Fear of mobs and the violence they bring appeared in Margaret's writings in later life.

In 1643 Margaret wanted to become a Lady in Waiting to Queen Henrietta-Maria, she had heard stories of how brave she was. When under fire from Parliamentarian warships in Yorkshire, she ran back to save her lapdog. The Queen called herself, "she majesty generalissima".

Margaret's reasons for this were mixed, she saw the Queen as a person made of the same stuff as herself, it was a career path she could follow, and it got her away from her home, with the chance to travel.

Ignoring her families pleas that she didn't know what she was doing and was too inexperienced in the ways of the world, she turned to pleading with her mother.

After getting her way, she left London secretly, to head for Oxford and the Queen. What Margaret didn't know as she headed out into the world that Summer, was that she would never see her mother again.

Oxford was now the Capital and military headquarters, weapons were being forged in the hallowed halls of academia, the University buildings were being changed to workshops, store houses and billets for the army.

She was, at twenty, in the middle of a world she didn't understand. She spent a considerable amount of her time standing behind the Queen, as the ladies in waiting added to her magnificence. She had to be completely still for hours. She found this difficult and often felt as if she was going to faint. Later in the day the court would come to life when the King arrived to visit. Then it was a glamorous job, in the middle of the top people of day, where rumour and gossip buzzed through the various cliques. The pretty witty Queen surrounded herself with like minded, sometimes vicious tongued friends.

Margaret was lost, she was quiet and studious, did not play cards, or take part in the witty banter, watched afraid of what the other ladies would say about her. Even though slandering others could ruin reputations of both men and women, it seemed to Margaret's young eyes, that they indulged in it anyway.

She kept out of it, catching no-one's eye, speaking very little. The war soon caught up with Oxford and the Court and on the 17th of April the Queen and her retinue left for the West Country.

The Queen gave birth to a daughter on this flight, and afterwards leaving the child in Exeter, they made for Falmouth and across the channel to France. The crossing was rough and they were chased by Parliamentarian ships firing at them. The heroic little Queen told the captain to blow up their ship rather than be captured. Margaret's thoughts were racing, she was in the hold with the other ladies, terribly seasick, frightened and thinking that her big career move would

"prove for my life to be unprofitably lost."

A storm blew their ship to Brittany, and the Queen and her retinue were welcomed once the French realised who they were. Margaret was covered in vomit and mud as she climbed up from the beach, so was everyone else, but they were on their way to Paris and the comfort of the court.

It was said that the ladies were so encrusted with vomit, mud and sea salt that they had to be cut out of their gowns.

Margaret hated the Paris court, she couldn't speak French, had no contact with her family, and worst of all got dysentery. Luckily Dr William Davison, the King's physician treated her and she recovered well.

In 1645 a middle aged Cavalier called William Cavendish, Marquess of Newcastle, arrived in Paris to pay his respects to the Queen. He was a very rich man. The son of Bess of Hardwick, an exceptional horseman with two great houses in England; Bolsover Castle in Derbyshire and Welbeck Abbey in Nottinghamshire. He had taught Charles to ride when he was a boy and was close to the Royal family, entertaining them frequently at his houses before the wars.

William Cavendish entertained King Charles and Queen Henrietta-Maria in this room at Bolsover Castle.(xiv)

He noticed the twenty two year old Margaret. He thought she was beautiful; tall, slender and quiet. He was distrustful of the court beauties and liked her because she was different. All the differences that made the other ladies dislike Margaret was exactly the reason he decided to court her.

The courtiers tried to break up their romance by telling the Queen well before the couple had married, that Margaret had married William in secret without the Queen's permission.

Henrietta-Maria was suspicious of Margaret and cold towards her, but when she found out it was gossip after Margaret spoke to her, she allowed them to marry in Paris in 1646.

To William, having a wife who wrote didn't worry him. Both his daughters from his first wife had written plays, and one of them Jane, was a Royalist spy.

Throughout their courtship and marriage William and Margaret wrote passionately to each other, they had fallen in love and remained in love with each other for the whole of their lives.

As many Royalists did,they became exiles in Paris, their money and lands claimed by Parliament in England. Most living in near poverty, relying on friends and servants to help them.

During this time Margaret came into her own, mending and re-mending worn out clothes. Buying cheap ribbons to dress up and change old garments. She became the centre of a literary group who admired her work. But all through this time together with William she was desperately worried about money.

Impoverished, fretting, but trying to cover it, to make matters worse she heard her mother Elizabeth died in her sleep, and her sister Mary died of consumption. Still the war raged on with atrocities on both sides it was becoming the accepted norm to give no quarter. By 1647 Margaret's health was failing, she began to make cures for the flux (dystentry) and become interested in chemistry.

They began to pawn some family items for food. Sir William met with his creditors and persuaded them to let them have money for necessary items, and Margaret sent to her brother John in England to ask for her Dowry money to be paid.

It was Henrietta-Maria who saved Margaret and William, repaying part of a debt he had loaned her five years previously. The grand sum of £2,000.

The personal loss was also great, the war had taken Margaret's brothers and in 1648 she became depressed thinking of their deaths. In other ways life was better, they had a good house to live in now and food and drink.

They both tried remedies for their childlessness. He took wood ash in his wine, and as always for women, the painful option, she had herbs injected into her womb.

Sad to say, it was probably William's womanising before he met Margaret that made him sterile. He probably caught some disease that affected him, he was also in his mid fifties. Though, as was the way of the world at the time, it was Margaret who was blamed for not providing an heir. It was always the woman's fault.

Although married for twenty years, they had no children of their own. Throughout the ups and downs of war, and in sickness and in health and for richer or poorer, they supported each other. Both suffered various illnesses, for which the cures were worse than the sickness. During this time Margaret became more interested in chemistry and mixing of nostrums and treating herself when the doctor's cures did not work immediately.

Their move to Antwerp brought them into bigger society, mathematicians, artists, writers, the upwardly mobile of 17th c society, but no people of their own class. William bought himself two horses and used them to practice his horsemanship.

Worse was to come in 1649, King Charles walked bravely to his beheading in Whitehall, wearing two shirts as it was a cold day and he did not want to shiver in case anyone thought he was scared to meet his maker.

Margaret's confidence grew and she was able to go and plead for her husband's sequestered lands from Parliament, as many wives did.

A strange aside here, a friend of mine, a medium, was visiting Bolsover Castle with her husband. As she walked through the rooms she stopped to talk to an old gentleman sitting on the guides chair by the door. He was dressed as a Cavalier, not that odd to her, as she had just been taking part in a Sealed Knot re-enactment and she was dressed as a 17thc lady. "Are you all right?" she asked him as he had his head in his hands. "I'm waiting for my brother mistress," he answered, "Tis my job to see to his household while he is gone, and I am so very tired."

It was then she realised she was talking to Charles Cavendish, she calmly said to him. "I think you can go now, he is safely home." She started to walk away to catch up with her husband, turned, but in a second he had gone.

To try and précis the life of a woman like Margaret Cavendish is almost impossible. But she deserves a place in this book. If it wasn't for women like her, the female of the sex would not have moved forward as fast as it has, we would have had no female writers, doctors, female scientists, or female academics.

Margaret's health deteriorated, but still she worked, mixing with people like Renee Descartes, and the great and good of the day.

Charles, William's brother died after a bout of flu and they both felt bereft. He had been their main support during their exile, looking after their assets while they were away.

In the meantime, William was trying to help Charles II to find ways to return to England to regain his throne, while Margaret was taxing herself with her writing and philosophical questions.

When the Restoration came Margaret and William Cavendish returned to England to claim their homes. Mixing again with polite society Margaret's chat was too masculine for most of their friends, as was her dress, she chose a knee length coat for riding which caused amusement and gossip.

Nowadays we think nothing of dress rules except perhaps the latest fashion but in Margaret's day everything was observed and commented on; her writing, speech, clothes, hairstyles, attitudes. She said it didn't bother her, but like every woman I'm sure there were moments when she wondered why she was being singled out for such attention.

She was the first woman to attend a meeting of the Royal Society in May 1667. There were protests from the all-male fellows - Pepys called it a scandal. Margaret was the wife of William Cavendish FRS, a member of one of the great aristocratic dynasties of British science. She knew many of the leading fellows, such as Robert Boyle and Thomas Hobbes. She witnessed several experiments of "colours, loadstones, microscopes" and was "full of admiration". She wrote later that she wished that she, although a woman, could work more with loadstones, and that one lifetime would not be enough to discover all she wanted to know.

Pepys, however,was more interested in her clothes calling them

"so antic and her deportment so unordinary".

She thought the fellows dry and boring, disagreeing vehemently with them on vivisection and wondered why women were excluded from learned bodies. She wrote a lively Memoir, in which she gave an interesting definition of poetry as "mental spinning", and it being useful to the scientific mind.

Margaret's health had never been good, not helped by the poisonous nostrums she had dosed herself with over the years. In modern parlance she wanted to “live fast and die young”.

Mostly she wanted to be remembered for her science-fiction novel, for her poetry and plays. She wasn't scared of death, she said that people who kept fit and dieted were wasting their lives as they were going to die anyway, they were just putting it off.

She also said that marriage is the grave or tomb of wit, it wasn't for her, but for many other women of her time it was.

She wanted to do as much as she could, ate to live, sat down too much, used her brilliant mind in everything she did, and had a loving supporting husband at her side.

She died on the 15th December 1673 at Welbeck, suddenly and without an obvious cause, aged 50. William arranged her funeral at Westminster Abbey, but at the age of 80 and unwell himself didn't attend, he died three years later in 1676.

They were buried together in Westminster Abbey.
Shall we leave the last few lines to William who said of Margaret

“she was a wise, witty, learned lady and a virtuous loving wife”

Gonzales Coques, "Portrait of a married couple in a park," or ´Lord Cavendish and his wife Margaret in the Rubens Garden in Antwerp` 1662 (Kat.Nr. 858). Staatliche Museen zu Berlin, Gemäldegalerie;

Foto: Jörg P. Anders. (xv)

Bolsover Castle, Derbyshire Home of the Newcastles (xvi)

Lucy Hutchinson

Lucy Hutchinson 1620-1681 (xvii)

Lucy was born to Sir Allen Apsley and Lady Lucy St John in the Tower of London where her father was Lieutenant. Lucy like Madge Newcastle was born to be a writer. She was a spoilt, but well educated Puritan child, and says herself that:

> *"my parents applied all their cares and spar'd no cost to improve me in my education"*

She was educated in both French and English, having a Frenchwoman for her nurse. By the time she was four she could read and write and was fluent in both languages. She remembered her father and mother carrying her to church to hear the sermons. She had such a good memory that she was able to repeat them at home exactly, for her reward she was tickled and kissed. She loved being praised, but she did not love music and needlework, the usual accomplishments of young ladies,

> *"as for my needle - I absolutely hated it" she wrote in later years.*

She loved reading which worried her mother, too much reading is bad for a women's health and marriage prospects! She also hated playing with other children, preferring to learn Latin from her father's chaplain.

She even preached to her mother's maids "to turn them good". I suspect the maid's thoughts were far from good, being preached to by a 9 year old was not part of their job description! Unfortunately Lucy also liked taking an interest in their love lives!

When Lucy was eighteen she met John Hutchinson, the son of Sir John Hutchinson of Owthorpe, another who, when a child, had been "serious above his years". The 23 year old John and Lucy seemed to have been made for each other, they fell in love in the Spring of 1638, and married in the July.

They both had a passionate love for one another, he said he loved her better than life, and she devoted herself to him.

> *"Soe as his shaddow, I waited on him everywhere until he was taken into that region of light which admitts none, then I vanisht into nothing."*

Four months into their marriage Lucy nearly lost her life when she miscarried twins. But the following year brought better news when she again gave birth to twins in September. Both the boys grew to adulthood.

In 1641 John disgusted his Royalist neighbours by defacing paintings in local churches and removing statues in the name of Puritanism. When the King's standard was raised at Nottingham John and his brother George joined the Parliamentarian cause with gusto preventing the ammunition store from being taken for the King's use.

It was at this time Lucy started writing everything down, giving us the best first-hand look at life during the English Civil War. She wrote her husband's biography "Memoirs of the Life of Colonel Hutchinson."

She gave us the information that :-

"when Puritanism grew into a faction, the zealots distinguished themselves both men and woemen, by severall affectations of habitt, lookes and words, cutting their haire close round their heads so that from this custom, that the name of Roundhead became the scornfull terme given to the whole Parliament Party."

However, it did not apply to all Puritans. Lucy describes her husband:-

"very ill applied to Colonel Hutchinson, who having fine thicksett head of haire naturally kept it cleane and handsome without any affectation, so that it was a greate ornament to him."

At one time when John was being chased by the King he ran away to Leicester. He had asked the pregnant Lucy to join him there, but as he arrived into the town he noticed that the Cavaliers were behind him so he rode out the other end. Lucy was left waiting to meet him in a strange house with George, her brother in law.

Soon a Captain Welch, who was a friend of her brother, came knocking at her door. He said it was a pity that she had a husband so unworthy of her that he was ashamed to be seen with her.

Lucy was so annoyed she decided to play a trick on the Captain, telling him he was mistaken and that her husband was not in hiding and could show his face where any honest man could.

"And to confirme to you, sayd she, he shall now come to you."

Lucy then called to her brother-in-law George who was in the house with her and ready to play her little game.

You have to bear in mind here, that without mobiles/social media etc., that only the rich and famous had portraits painted, and these were well known, so that this sort of thing could happen very easily.

Captain Welch was shocked, and said as he was in his wife's parlour he would not arrest John Hutchinson. He went away perplexed. Lucy and George had a good laugh at their joke, they thought the Cavaliers had moved away and that they were safe. But Captain Welch returned and arrested George as his brother John. Lucy tried to explain it was a joke and George wasn't her husband but her brother-in-law. Captain Welch had been humiliated enough for one day and his Dragoons took George away probably just to spite the pair.

It was only when George was taken to Prince Rupert that he was identified as the other brother. But it took Lucy begging her cousin, Viscount Grandison, who was serving in the Kings Army to intervene and get him freed. Lucy's family were fighting on both sides of the divide - as were lots of families during the war.

During the siege of Nottingham Castle she helped the Governor's wife attend to the wounded, even the Royalists. One of the more zealous Parliamentarian soldiers said he hated to see her helping the enemy, but Lucy said she was helping all God's creatures, as men, not enemies.

Lucy had nine children during her lifetime, translated Lucretius's texts on "The Nature of Things" into English from Latin and documented hers and her husband's lives in her "Memoirs", written for her children. I couldn't find the names of the twins, but only of one son named John for his father.

After the war at the Restoration, John Hutchinson was one of the few men who signed the King's Death-warrant who was arrested but not tried. He was imprisoned in Sandown Castle in Kent, and Lucy pleaded at the House of Lords for him to be freed but it was refused and he died in prison. Lucy died in 1681 aged 60.

Anne Fanshawe

Anne Fanshawe 1625-1680 (xviii)

The Devils Whore? I don't think so.

Anne Fanshawe would have be devastated to think this was what the 21st Century thought of her. Unfortunately, a lot of people thought this historical television fiction programme was the truth and so I am going to set the record straight for Anne as she can't speak for herself. This is her true life story, which is so amazing in itself that it doesn't need to be dramatised any further.

Anne was born in London on 25 March 1625 to Margaret Fanshawe and Sir John Harrison. She had three brothers and a younger sister, growing up sharing their childhood between the two family houses in London and Hertford. She learnt to speak French, play the lute and virginals (a small harpsichord), was good with all kinds of fine needlework, and could cook. Anne loved outdoor sports especially riding and running, and other active pastimes. In today's world, she would be at yoga and spin class and aerobics, as well as holding down a full-time job.
In her Memoirs she described herself with hindsight as :

"what we graver people call a hoyting girle."

Anne's father was a wealthy Royalist, in fact one of the richest men in England at the time. Her mother died in July 1640 when Anne was 15, and she took over the management of her father's house in Bishopsgate Street in London. Saying it was time to:

"put away those little childnesses."

It was also in 1640 her father remarried, he obviously felt that to wait a year's mourning was unnecessary. His new wife very quickly giving birth to a son and a daughter.

In 1642 Anne's' life was to change drastically, her father and brother William left Parliament to side with the King with her father John making a large contribution to the Royal purse. His reward from his colleagues in Parliament was to arrest him, sequester his lands and money, and order him to be transported to the West Indies.

But John escaped on some pretence of getting some paperwork that Parliament had demanded to see concerning the public revenue. So it was that the family arrived in Oxford, destitute and suffering from shock, their London house had been looted and ransacked.
Anne writes

"we had untill that houre lived in greate plenty and greate order, we found ourselves fishes out of water, for from as good houses as any gentleman in England had we came to a baker's house in an obscure street, from roomes well furnished to lie in a very bad bed in a garrett, to one dish of meat and that not the best ordered, for we were as poor as Job, nor clothes more than man or two brought in our cloak bags."

Anne thought that she might have to live in a tent for the rest of her life. As poor as life was in Oxford Anne was not expecting another disaster to follow so quickly. Her brother William had his horse shot out from under him by Essex's cavalry and died from the fall.

"He was very good and gallant young man."

Anne wrote in her diary the same words that the King had said of William when he heard he had died.

At the age of 18 she married a distant cousin, Sir Richard Fanshawe. The wedding was held in Wolvercote Church. Only a few friends and relatives attended as the war and probably finances prevented anything bigger. She was given her mother's wedding ring to wear, by her father, which was his first wife's wish.

The couple started married life with just £20 between them. Richard was a career diplomat. They had 14 children over their life together, four daughters and only one son lived to maturity and it was for him she wrote her memoirs. They never had a settled home, but they had a very happy marriage and Richard doted on her.

In March 1645 Richard was charged with taking the 14 year old Prince Charles to Bristol to set up his own court. It was the first time the couple had ever been apart and the timing couldn't have been worse. Anne had just given birth to their first child, and she didn't want to be alone. The baby was weak and sickly. Unusually, Sir Richard himself was tearful at leaving his little family in a garrison town. Sadly their little boy died two days after his father left.

Anne herself felt extremely weak and ill, it took until May till she felt strong enough to leave her room and go to church. After the service a gentleman approached her and gave her a letter from her husband and 50 pieces of gold. The letter said that Richard wanted her to join him in Bristol.

It was shortly after that, that Anne was nearly shot by accident. She rushed to tell her father her good news. They could hear drums coming down the street outside St John's College and they went up the mound to see the soldiers march by. It turned out it was Sir Charles Lee's Company of Foot, a friend of theirs. He saw them standing underneath a tree on the mound and decided to give his friends a volley of shot as a compliment. The musket balls splintered the tree trunk about 2 inches above Anne's head!

A couple of days Later Anne started off to go to Bristol and meet her husband feeling better just at the thought of it.
"little thought I to leap into that sea that tossed me till it racked me."
She wrote later after 25 years of adventures abroad. Richard was very happy to see her, he took her in his arms, and then presented her with the rest of his gold. (My kind of man!) Saying he wanted her to keep his fortune for him and he will increase it with God's blessing.

Richard was happy to share his gold with Anne. But not state secrets, although she pestered him to share, egged on by Countess Rivers. She told Anne that she knew that some letters had arrived from Queen Henrietta for the King, and she wanted Anne to tell her what was in them. Anne followed him into his study asking to see his papers. Richard told her that it was his job, not hers, and told her to go away as he was very busy. Anne was not speaking to him at dinner and refused to eat, Anne sulked and cried while Richard slept. The next day Richard kissed her goodbye on his way to work and she still refused to speak to him. In the evening she said to him that he didn't care for her, to see her so troubled. He took her in his arms and said:

> *"My dearest soule, nothing on earth can afflict me like that; and when you asked me of my busines, it is wholy out of my power to satisfy thee. For my life and fortune shall be thine, and every thought of my heart, but my honour is my own and I cannot communicate the Prince's affaires, and pray thee with this answer rest satisfied."*

Anne realised how stupid she's been to listen to Countess Rivers, and never asked Richard to share work confidences again.

The plague was racking Bristol and so the court moved to Barnstaple in Devon. Anne thought it was the best place they had seen, mainly because she enjoyed the Devon cherry pies and cream and made friends with a 100 year old parrot in the house where they found lodgings.

As Cromwell moved into the West Country the young Prince Charles fled to the Scilly Isles and the Fanshawe's had to follow. Anne had to put all they had into two trunks to escape on the frigate - The Phoenix - which was waiting at Falmouth. Unfortunately they had put themselves in the hands of pirates, the ship was commanded by a Sir Nicholas Crispe, and although Richard tried to pay the pirates off with gold, during the night the seamen broke into their trunks and helped themselves to Anne's money and clothes. Once again she was destitute.

When they arrived in the Scilly Isles, Anne pregnant, seasick and needing to sleep, found she was billeted in the lowest of low rooms. She went to bed and woke up to find the bed floating as the tide had come in. The landlord was not surprised as he said it always happened at Spring tide. They found themselves begging for what little food they could get, but it was generally bad and not enough.

There was a story, I don't know if it was true, that I heard while living in Cornwall, that it was in this house that Anne saw a ghost. She saw a women who was grey and transparent moaning out of a window towards the harbour with her arms outstretched. Anne was terrified thinking she was either going mad, or it was a bad omen.

After three weeks of this torture they managed to get to the Loyal Island of Jersey, where they were entertained in the style to which they were accustomed in the grand houses. The people were cheerful and Anne and Richard stayed with a widow, Madame de Pommes in St Helier. It was there that Anne gave birth to a daughter who they had to leave behind in the care of Lady Carteret's nurse so that they could see the young Prince Charles safely to his mother in Paris.

The Civil war was over at last. The couple spent their life together travelling across Europe with Richard's job as a diplomat to Caen, Paris, The Hague, Ireland, Madrid, and Flanders as well as London, Yorkshire, Huntingdonshire, Hertfordshire and Bath.

Richard continued with his publishing of translations and keeping the Royal family up to date with developments abroad. Anne followed wherever Richard was posted, she loved him so much, she had built her world around him.

Richard was posted to Portugal to help arrange the marriage of Charles II to Catherine of Braganzia. Anne gave birth to a son, her last child and her only surviving boy there. Richard served as ambassador to Portugal and to Spain until 1666.

In 1666 in Madrid Richard died aged 58. Anne decided to bring Richard's body back to England accompanied by her baby son, her four daughters all under the age of 13 years and thirty servants. She sold her plate and had been given £2000 by the Spanish Queen and was proud to say she left without being a penny in debt

"Which every embassador cannot say."

The redoubtable and faithful Anne arrived in England to be welcomed by her family.

You have to bear in mind that this woman travelled over the landscape of Portugal, Spain and France with her husband's body wrapped up and being pulled on a donkey cart. She had a baby and three teenage daughters to look after, which any mother today knows would not make any journey easy. She was almost robbed by highwaymen on this journey, and she with her entourage managed to fight them off, which must have been tiresome to say the least.

On the 23rd November Anne was received by the King who greeted her cordially enough and listened to her adventures, Charles II promised to take care of her and her family and to repay the £6000 that Richard had spent on his behalf as an ambassador, and make sure that she received his pay.

Anne had to wait three years for the money, and even then, it was £2000 short and Richards salary was never paid. Once again Anne was poverty stricken and having to adjust to living on very little. She missed Richard dreadfully and felt that after all they'd been through on behalf of the King she should have been better treated. She was at a very low ebb, but she decided to get her life back for the sake of her children, who were all still very young and needed her.

Ten years after Richard's death in 1676, Anne wrote his Memoir for their son Richard. It described Richard's character to his son, it gives descriptions of their travels, the people they met and their adventures together.

Anne Fanshawe has also left her cookery books and one of them has the earliest recipe for ice cream to be made dated 1651.

Here is one of her recipes:
Recipe for Sugar Cakes :

> *"Take 2 pound of Butter, one pound of fine Sugar, the yolkes of nine Egs, a full Spoonfull of Mace beat & searsed [sifted], as much Flower as this will well wett making them so stiffe as you may rowle it out, then with the Cup of a glasse of what Size you please cutt them into round Cakes & pricke them and bake them."*

Anne Fanshaw was an amazing intelligent and loving woman. She had so many strengths to survive what the 17thc world had thrown at her. Knocked down many times to jump straight back up and start again.

Anne died on 20th January 1680 aged 55 and is buried near her family home in Ware parish church beside her beloved husband.

I hope I've put the record straight - never mind Devil's Whore - to me Anne Fanshawe you will always be Superwoman.

Prepare to Fly: The Witches of the 17th Century

Hey How for Hallowene
All the witches to be seen,
Some in black and some in green,
Hey How for Hallowene

Old Scots Rhyme

It has never been a good time to be a witch and during the Civil War was no exception. Charles' father, James the first of Scotland and England, made it his duty to follow the Bible when it said, "Thou shalt not suffer a witch to live". He was a well known misogynist and homosexual, although in these aspects he chose not to practice what the Bible preached.

King James had written a Daemonologie, published in 1599. This was a book on how to find witches and how to recognise and punish them. He had already taken a personal interest in the Berwick witch trials. He approved of witch hunting, to quote him

"that the instrument thereof (the witch) merits most severely to be punished."

There must have been a sigh of relief amongst ordinary village women when James died. Wise women who knew how to cure coughs and colds, bind up cuts with herbs so that they wouldn't fester, make love potions to rise men up, could now prepare their potions and medicines with a little less fear.

There was a fine line between being a good housewife (a Goodwyfe) and being a cunning women.

A Goodwyfe had many duties; to make salves and preserves, to see to the health and well being of the family and the servants, to run her year to an Almanack of months, to keep accounts as best she could, and to instruct and manage the household according to her Lord's needs and wants.

A cunning woman was usually paid for her services and had usually been taught how to make politices and potions by her mother. The recipes that worked would be passed down through the generations. She would have lived in the village where most of the inhabitants were superstitious and uneducated.

She could also be a midwife, although there was a danger in this, she may be accused of killing the child or even worse swapping it for a changling. All midwives had to have a certificate signed by at least nine other women and issued by the town officials before they could practice.

It was believed by most men that women had always been lustful. Unable to control their venial feelings, they were the ones leading men into revolution and revolt. These daughters of Eve, these dangerous creatures, had to be bridled and kept under control. Witches were in league with the Devil, their lust satisfied by having sex with him. Powers were given in exchange for doing this work.

Women were not to be trusted ever since Eve tempted Adam with the apple from the Tree of Knowledge. Women were necessary to stop men from turning to sin and for the procreation of children, but they were also dangerous, so the rhetoric tells the 17th Century husband.

Add to this mix the self-styled Witchfinder General Matthew Hopkins. His career took off during the English Civil War. His witch-hunts mainly took place in the puritan counties of Suffolk, Essex, and Norfolk, though it is known he travelled far and wide for his business. There is a pub on the seafront in Penzance, Cornwall, called the Dolphin which dubiously posts it's claim to fame that it's upper rooms had been used by Matthew Hopkins to conduct his "trials."

He started his witch hunts in March 1644 and in three years he and his helpers probably had more women tortured and hanged for witchcraft than in the previous 100 years or more. It's said he was personally responsible for the deaths of around 300 witches between the years 1644 and 1646. I imagine some men were in this number and died as warlocks. Matthew Hopkins had worked for John Stearne, who was a witch-hunter. However, as Matthew Hopkins had more charisma and had styled himself Witch Finder General, he turned the tables employing John Stearne to help him with his considerable workload.

Ten years earlier, following the Lancaster Witch Trial of 1634, William Harvey, King Charles' doctor, had been ordered to examine the four women accused, he was looking for proof positive. So Matthew Hopkins employed women called Prickers to look for the proof they needed to convict the women.

Witches were supposed to suckle their master the Devil, any woman who had an extra nipple, or a hanging wart on her body, or any red marks or birth marks were singled out as being a witch.

The accused women were often stripped naked, shaved of all body hair, their hands tied above their heads so that they could not perform a spell, and inspected closely for such marks. Sometimes by other women from their village, sometimes by the men in charge of the village, or by women employed as Prickers. Humiliating for the poor women involved. If any of these marks were found the women were tortured until they confessed.

In his book The Discovery of Witches, Hopkins claimed he became a witch-finder when he apparently listened to women discussing their meetings with the Devil in March 1644. What actually motivated him, I imagine, was the free pass to travel the country in the middle of the Civil War that he and Stearne received from the superstitious puritans. They would also have been encouraged by the 20 shillings they were paid by the grateful villagers for ridding their villages of witches (around £3000 in todays money). Apparently this was to pay for his assistants and their horses, he cheekily also charged travelling expenses.

Luckily for the women living at that time Matthew Hopkins had a short life, he died aged about 25 years old. There is a story that someone had asked him, "How did he know so much about witches? To know so much surely he must be one!" He decided to retire at this and died at his home of TB shortly afterwards.

For a book about women in the English Civil War, I have spent the last few pages on one evil man which wasn't really meant to happen. So after these next few paragraphs I promise I'll get back onto the women proper.

One woman was saved by her local preacher John Gaule, vicar of Great Staughton. He had heard a woman was being held charged with witchcraft waiting in jail until Matthew Hopkins could come. Matthew Hopkins wrote to St Neots to ask if he could be expect a "good welcome". John heard of his letter, and published Select Cases of Conscience touching Witches and Witchcrafts; in London, (1646). He also began a series of Sunday sermons to suppress witch-hunting in the Cambridgeshire area. Matthew Hopkins and company did not arrive and the woman was set free.

It seems that most village women who were accused of witch-craft were thought to put curses on cows so they wouldn't milk, or crops so that they would die of disease.

When I lived in Cornwall, I found out there was a witch called Old Meggie in the St Just area in the 1640s who was paid by sailors to sit on the rocks and whistle up the wind so that their ships were no longer becalmed.

These were natural phenomenon that occurred from time to time, but to the 17th century mind somebody was behind it.

In earlier days, witches like Mother Shipton of Knaresborough, Yorkshire in the 1500s were part of village life. Mother Shipton was a seer and predicted the Great Fire of London in 1666, she made remedies and potions from the herbs and flowers in the forest where she lived.

In James 1st's day, The Pendle Witch trials were held on the evidence of a nine year old child. Jennet Device, who when she was 16, had the tables turned against her, and she herself was accused of witchcraft. She was not punished properly, for although the child caused ten people to be hung, her mother, her grandmother and some of their friends included, at the time the courts were merciful. She was not hung, but acquitted and asked to pay for the time she spent in jail. The last she was heard of was in 1636, nine years before the Civil War started, she then disappeared from history.

Apparently a 350-year-old notebook, documenting the trials of women convicted of witchcraft in England during the 17th Century by an English Puritan named Nehemiah Wallington has been found. The manuscript is one of Wallington's seven surviving notebooks. The woodturner wrote 50 journals about religion, the civil war and witchcraft trials during the course of his life.

He gives details of a witchcraft trial held in Chelmsford in July 1645. "Some Christians have been killed by their meanes," he states.
He must have attended the trial as an onlooker. What follows has been borrowed with thanks and adapted from:
www. witchtrials.co.uk/west.html where you can read the whole trial and result.
I have translated the following from the Early Modern English.

Rebecca confessed, that on Shrove Tuesday last her mother told her to hurry up and finish her work and go with her before sundown to a meeting, as they were going over the fields, her mother told her not to speak of anything she heard or saw that night, Rebecca agreed.

When they came to the meeting house, there were five Witches there; two chiefs were Mother Benefield and Mother Goodwin, she took out a Book which they prayed from. Then several Imps appeared in the shape of Kittens about a week old on Mother Benefield's lap, she kissed them, and told Rebecca that they were her children which she had by as handsome a man as any in England.

Then they called on their Spirits come to kill a horse, a cow, a child, then Mother Benefield called to Mother West, and asked if she were sure that her daughter Rebecca keep quiet, she was told Rebecca had promised.

They replied, if she ever did speak of it that they'd make sure she would suffer torture and pain on earth, then the pain of hell. Mother Benefield asked her to take the Covenant and Oath. They taught her what to say, to deny God and Saviour

Jesus Christ, to renounce all promises of his blessings and to believe as they did, serve and obey as they did.

Rebecca confessed that as soon as she had done this, the Devil in the shape of a little black dog leaped into her lap, & kissed her three times, she felt very cold. Shortly after, when she was going to bed, the Devil appeared unto her again in the shape of a handsome young man, saying that he came to marry her.

I take thee Rebecca to be my wife, and do promise to be thy loving husband till death, defend you from all harm; then he told her what she must say, whereupon she took him by the hand and said, I Rebecca take thee to be my husband, and do promise to be an obedient wife till death, faithfully to perform and observe all thy commands. She was asked by the Judge whether she ever had carnal copulation with the Devil, she confessed that she had.

After being asked several questions by a Gentleman that spoke to her several times with her giving her godly and comfortable advice, she agreed that as soon as one of the Witches was in prison, she would confess all she knew, which she did. The other witches were caught and sent Jail.

She affirmed, that when she was going to the Grand Inquest with Mother Miller (indicted for a Witch) she told Mother Miller that she would confess nothing. Even if they pulled her to pieces with pincers: and being asked the reason by the Gentleman, she said she found herself in such extremes of torture and amazement, that she would not endure it again for the world. When she looked on the ground she saw herself covered in flames of fire.

When presently the Grand Inquest called for her, where they admit one at a time, as soon as she was separated from Mother Miller, the tortures and the flames stopped. So she confessed all she knew, and said that so soon as her confession over, she found herself unburdened of all her tortures, she felt happy.

We will never know what happened to this young girl, it seems the women were in some sort of cult and she was drawn in. A dangerous place to be, for Rebecca there was escape this time, but not for many others.

The 17th Century was not the place to be if you were the type of person who had to try and do something about your way of life and use witch-craft to try and force a change for the better. It was also not for innocent women who knew too much about herbs, or who mumbled swear words or curses to people who'd upset them, and were overheard. Or lonely women who kept cats and dogs for company and spoke to them, or sometimes for women who were just in the wrong place at the wrong time.

The She Soldiers of the Civil War

She-soldiers of the Sealed Knot marching off to fight in Nantwich (xix)

From the song of The Gallant She Soldier.

With musket on her shoulder, her part she acted then
And everyone supposed that she had been a man;
Her bandoleers about her neck, and sword hang'd by her side
In many brave adventures her valour have been tried.

Throughout the English Civil War there were women fighting dressed as men in the rank and file. The Royalist Armies had the biggest contingent of women in the ranks. King Charles knew about this and tried to put a stop to it, he believed that the women were only there to ply their trade as whores amongst the soldiers. Possibly nothing could have been further from the truth as some Armies already had whores who travelled with them. If not, the soldiers visited local bawdy houses when they reached towns and villages.

Many women picked up their dead husbands coats and fought in their stead, they were fed and paid, sometimes. For many of them, there was nothing to go home for. Their homes and crops had been destroyed and their animals stolen, both Armies were guilty of this and left a trail of devastation in their wake. But for the most part it was just to keep the wolf from the door.

Although both sides had similar regulations, the Royalists did not enforce them to the letter. They tended to turn a blind eye against a good female soldier; not so the Parliamentarians. Nearly all the known she-soldiers fighting in the first Civil War (1642-46) were Royalists, many of them were in the cavalry.

A mixed troupe of Sealed Knot Royalist and Roundhead Cavalry with the King in the centre (xx)

Perhaps it was easier to be a cavalry trooper to hide her sex, the clothing was heavy and hid a women's shape well, unless in hand to hand fighting. The cavalry was usually seen from a distance. On the field, the Commander could see a lot less of the cavalry than the infantry.

It was extremely hard to find much evidence of women soldiers. Hardly surprising as most of them hid under male names, sometimes of their husbands or brothers who had been lost in the action.

In a recent survey of the current Sealed Knot membership it was found that the Parliamentarians had the most same sex couples and the Royalists had the most illegitimate children, but interestingly no one counted how many women were fighting as soldiers on either side. So it is the same today as it has always been.

One of the earliest mentions of a she-soldier was in July 1645, when a Parliamentarian news sheet told of the capture of a female soldier who had been following her lover.

In March 1645, Royalist cavalry from Lord Percy's Regiment made an unsuccessful raid on Cromwell's troops in Andover and many were taken prisoner. One of whom was 'a youth of so fair a countenance' that Cromwell was intrigued by this. For his amusement he ordered the 'young man' to sing, it was obvious by his voice, that he was in fact a woman. The story of Anne Dymock, another female soldier, follows later in the book, and only differs in the fact that she was one of the few women who fought for Parliament.

Trooper Lady Jane Ingilby

Ripley Castle (xxi)

The Ingilbys were an ancient Yorkshire family dating from 1090. It was in 1308/9 when Sir Thomas Ingilby married his wife Edeline Thwenge that Ripley Castle came to the family as part of Edeline's dowry.

The family moved through the centuries, always close to the Crown, the Kings and Queens of England.

The Inglebys were a staunchly Catholic family and they decided to fight for the King and his Catholic wife Henrietta-Maria during the English Civil War. Only 58 years earlier they were plotting to remove Elizabeth I from the throne and also involved in the gunpowder plot to blow up Parliament and

James VI of Scotland - the father of King Charles, the man they were now fighting for.

The family were always in the centre of the events of the day, fighting for what they believed in.

During my research I asked why there was no portrait of Lady Jane Ingleby or Trooper Ingleby as she was known. When Jane was a child her family nickname was Captain, so I imagine she was a tomboyish little girl with a mind of her own.

I was told that some of the Inglebys were very good looking and some were not, it was a generational thing. Some of those who were not good looking in a time when your face really could be your fortune, preferred not to have their portraits painted. For example Lady Jane's nephew, young Sir William, who was not particularly good looking, had to employ the services of a match-maker to help him find a wife.

Jane was the third child of Sampson and Jane Ingilby born in Ripley Castle on the 3rd April 1601. She seemed to be an adventurous woman. She disguised herself as a man and went to fight on horseback with her older brother Sir William Ingleby at Marston Moor. She would have had to have been trained how to fight with sword on horseback and it was probably her brother who taught her.

Jane had just had her 43rd birthday on the 3rd of April 1644 when she rode out to fight with her brother Sir William.

A storm was brewing and not just amongst the troops on the battlefield. It was a close, hot day with thunderclouds boiling overhead when the Ingilbys rode out to join Prince Rupert of the Rhine on the battlefield. It was clear from the start that the Royalists were outnumbered.

Jane and her brother sat on horseback all day in the heat and rain waiting for the action to start. The day was spent marshalling armies who had been ready to retreat. The Royalists at last managed to get 17,500 men (and women) on the field, the Parlimentarians had 27,000. Between the armies was a deep ditch - the ground was chosen to unhorse the cavalry when the battle began.

By 4 o'clock no-one had made a move. Parliament thought to rush the Royalists instead of waiting for them to charge forward but nothing happened.

The photograph above was taken at one of our Sealed Knot re-enactments at Newstead Abbey. The Cavalier behind the King with the red ostrich feather is a female showing how Lady Jane could disguise herself as a man.(xxii)

Jane must have been extremely hot and uncomfortable, the layers she was wearing would have been; breast bindings, a shirt, over which was worn a singlet (a type of waistcoat without arms), slips - a loose underbreech tied at the waist, then her woollen uniform breeches and hose (long over the knee length stockings), her legs protected by long leather bucket boots with lace ties. Her bucket boots are still at Ripley Castle, they look to be a size 3 or 4. So she wasn't a tall woman.

She was probably wearing a Buff coat (a yellowish buffalo skin, heavy three quarter length jacket) with a metal breastplate over the top. On top of that she would have her baldric with her sword hanging at her side, her felt hat which would probably have held a "secret", which was a metal helmet lined with padded linen, hidden under the hat to protect her head from sword blows.

She may have had a musket and pistols, and of course a water holder, a piss pot, and a snapsack which was a sort of shoulder bag made of leather or coarse linen that held food or anything else she needed. Wearing all this she was still willing to fight the enemy when the time came.

She must have been a very strong woman. If we can try and gather anything about her looks, we must look at the portraits of the family that do exist. Her father's portrait shows a strong broad face with a small flat nose, (her brother William's tomb effigy shows he looked very much like his father), whereas her mother had an oval face with a long nose, whether she took after her father or her mother we will never know, but what they both gave her was the strength and determination to be herself and to take fate into her own hands.

At 7pm it was decided by the Royalists that there was no fighting to be done that day, and it must have been with relief that the Cavalry turned their horses to the rear to loosen their saddles and girths and prepare to feed their horses and to eat their own evening meal.

The cooking pots were smoking and they were looking forward to the usual night at the camp, eating, drinking, taking their ease and talking and joking round the camp-fires about the days events.

It was the moment the Parliamentarians were waiting for - a cannon boomed sending a smoke ring and sparks into the air and the Battle of Marston Moor had begun. Everywhere the Royalist army rushed to get into their ranks ready to fight, but the surprise attack had allowed the Parliament horses to cross the deep ditch without being shot at by Royalist musket.

The opposing sides were so evenly matched that they fought themselves to a standstill. The Cavalry, of which Jane was a part, were hacking at each other with their swords until they were exhausted.

A group of Royalist soldiers decided to make a run for it, but were quickly brought back into the battle by being sworn at by Prince Rupert, more scared of him than Cromwell they fought on. When it became obvious there was no more they could do, the Royalists retreated.

Jane and William had been fighting for two hours and they must have been physically at the end of what their bodies could cope with, but fear of capture and the relative nearness of their home and safety made them gallop as fast as their horses could carry them back to Ripley Castle. The bodies they rode through were being stripped naked, the moans of the wounded men and cries of the dying horses were ringing in their ears. Alongside that the Parliament army were singing hymns and psalms in victory as they made their way back to their camps to dress their wounds and eat while 4,150 Royalist dead and around 1000 Roundheads' bodies littered the rye fields.

Hurtling through the darkness, exhausted, they arrived home at Ripley Castle. Frustratingly they were not immediately recognised and the door was not opened for them. Once safe inside their home, the brother and sister realised that Oliver Cromwell was hot on their heels. There was a high possibility that William would be ransomed or shot, so he went and hid in the heavily disguised Priest hole, leaving Jane to deal with Cromwell.

His sister must have, with the help of her maid, quickly turned herself back into Lady Jane. The list of mens clothing is a lot easier to take off than put on. A shift, a kind of long linen smock can be put over slips and hose, and a back lacing dress is easy to put on with the help of a maid.

By the time Oliver Cromwell was hammering at the door demanding rest and food, he was to be met by the lady of the house holding a pistol. Lady Jane at first refused him and his troops entry, swearing she had the means to defend the house against him. After some negotiation the troops and their prisoners were allowed to use the stables and Oliver Cromwell was allowed to sit in the Library, where Lady Jane held him at pistol point for the whole of the night. She sat opposite the General with her pistol trained on him. She did not even allow him to get up to use the pot or commode.

Cromwell was so badly accommodated at Ripley Castle that there is a local story which says, as soon as he was released from his captivity he raced down the lane to the nearest cottage, and in the front garden of Red Cat Cottage he relieved himself for a goodly while before moving on.

Tired and exhausted as she was Jane must have felt sick that her enemy Cromwell and his troops that she had been fighting on the bloody field of Marston Moor had been in her house.

It must have seemed like a punishment to her, when his troops took their Royalist prisoners and shot them against the gatehouse and east wall of her church. The musket holes are still there to this day. See below.

Musket ball holes in Ripley Church (xxiii)

Cromwell was known for his brutality and he did not keep prisoners or his own wounded soldiers long if they were likely to hold him back. Jane's bravery had saved her brother's life.

The fact that a mere woman, and a Royalist woman at that, had held Cromwell against his will, was hushed up. After winning the greatest battle of his life, to be held at pistol point by Lady Jane Ingilby did nothing to enhance the General's reputation. So Cromwell made sure it was kept quiet.

The priesthole that helped save William's life that night had been lost through time and only discovered again in 1964, and can now been seen at Ripley.

Jane died unmarried, at the age of 50 on the 20th December 1651, only seven years after the Battle of Marston Moor. For those seven years she continued living at the Castle and little is known of her during that time. She is buried in the church there. When I asked where she had been buried I was told that her grave has been lost over the years.

We know so little of this woman who fought as a soldier on horseback at the side of her elder brother, but what we do know is that what she may have lacked in beauty she more than made up for in bravery, endurance and integrity.

Anyway beauty is in the eye of the beholder - have you seen Cromwell warts and all?

Anne Dymock
Parliamentarian Soldier

When Anne Dymock fell in love with John Evison, I don't suppose for one moment she thought it would mean joining the Parliamentarian Army. She met John after her mother and father died and she was sent to live with her aunt a long way from home. John was Lincolnshire born and bred as was Anne and they must have had a lot in common, meeting as two strangers in a foreign county.

John loved Anne as much as she loved him and as they wanted to arrange their marriage they asked permission of her remaining family and friends, it was refused. John had no money to support a wife.

The couple couldn't bear to be apart so John and Anne eloped to London with Anne in disguise. By dressing as a man she passed herself off as John's brother Stephen. To earn their keep they decided to both join the Parliament Army and they fought together for two years side by side.

From what I can gather, after serving in the army they went into service, and in 1657 John and Stephen took a sea voyage to Scotland with their master during which John was washed overboard during a storm and died.

The ship put to port in the North of England and Anne, still dressed as Stephen, arrived in Carlisle wondering what to do. She was bereaved and knew no-one in Carlisle. She decided to take her dead lover's name and enlist in the peace-time army of Cromwell's Protectorate.

She served for many years under Major Tolhurst, and ended up serving in a garrison in Ayr where she remained undiscovered. It was Col. Roger Sawrey, the garrison commander who later said, when she was found out, that he

> *"... could not see anything but modesty from her when she was with us. Her work as a soldier was satisfatory."*

Kit Carrington
First Female Chelsea Pensioner

This next story is about a female soldier that took place about 40 or 50 years after the English Civil War. I thought that Kit's story was too good not to be told, so I hope you'll forgive me, and raise a tankard to her in the beer tent anyway.

After the Civil War, a *Mrs Christian Davies ran an ale house with her husband. She had two children and her mother-in-law lived with them to help with the children and the pub. Christian was of Irish descent as was her husband Richard Walsh.

In 1691, her husband disappeared after a night's drinking in his own ale house, having accidentally taken the Kings' shilling. The King's recruiters would pay a shilling to any man who would join them and, if there were unwilling recruits, they would put a shilling in the bottom of their tankard and, as soon as they choked on it, or held it in their hand, they were deemed to have taken the King's shilling whether they wanted to join the army or not.

Once Christian realised what had happened, she cut her hair, put on her husbands clothes and left her children with her mother-in-law to go in search of her husband.
She changed her name to Kit Carrington, hid her breasts by binding them under her husband's waistcoat and joined the English Army. She served as an infantryman, making a leather penis so that she could relieve herself against the trees before a battle like all the other men, so no one noticed that she was a female.

At the battle of Landen she was wounded and taken prisoner by the French she managed to keep everyone from both sides fooled and was exchanged without either side realising she was a woman.

Kit was discharged from the Army after a killing a man in a duel, but promptly signed up again as a dragoon, a member of the Cavalry.

She looked for her husband in the rank and file for thirteen years, during which she fought and caroused with the soldiers. In one town, she was even accused of fathering a child with a prostitute! Kit paid for the child to be brought up rather than give away her secret.

When Kit finally found her husband, he had taken another wife. He agreed to keep her identity hidden. I suppose she agreed to keep his bigamy quiet, and they both went back to their regiments and fighting the war.

At the battle of Ramillies in 1706 she was wounded again and this time it was discovered that she was a woman. She was so highly regarded by the Army that they continued to pay her and she took on the role of Sutler, providing the soldiers with food and drink, clothes and bedding.

In September 1709, she found out that her husband had been killed in the Battle of Malplaquet, and she again went to find him, apparently turning bodies over for two days on the battlefield to find him and give him a decent burial.

I hope Kit found some happiness with her second and third husbands, she didn't seem to give up on marriage despite how badly Richard, the husband she had loved so much, had treated her. Kit was so well thought of that she became the first female Chelsea Pensioner. She was buried with full military honours.

** I found that lots of women who were called Mrs, such as Mrs Christian Davies above, kept their unmarried names with the name Mrs to designate their married status. It doesn't follow in all cases, so I am led to believe it was personal choice.*

HEROICK LADYES

Sealed Knot Lady drummers at Naseby Battlefield waiting to go on (xxiv)

Throughout the Civil War, women were never far from the action, if they weren't involved in it, they were pretty sure it would be coming to them soon. As there was not much in the way of contraception, most married women would be pregnant every other year until their menopause. If they survived the birth of their children they went back to tending their households and businesses, also caring for their looks, their health, and their clothes. Bear this in mind as you read about the following ladies and their exploits.

London: The fortifications were thrown up hurriedly with the assistance of many women including the Lady Mayoress who brought her own tools, causing Samuel Butler to write:

"From ladies down to oyster wenches, Labour'd like pioneers in the trenches."

Bristol 1643: Mary Smith took food out to the men on the earthworks. Joan Batten and Dorothy Hazzard helped stop up (barricade) Frome Gate. 200 women went to the Parliamentarian Commander Colonel Fiennes offering to place themselves in front of the cannon to ward off shot.

Lyme, Dorset 1643: The women of Lyme successfully repelled the Royalist attack mounted by Prince Maurice, it was a bloody endeavour. Lyme was not prepared for this kind of attack. Prince Maurice was so confident he said he would take the town before breakfast - an hour's battle at most. It actually took weeks. The women would collect cannon balls from the beach in their aprons and bring them back for their own cannon to fire. The defenders of Lyme totalled around a thousand and they were poor fishermen and women, half of them had no shoes or hose. It didn't stop them defending their town. It was such a violent defence that at one point the water supply was running red with blood because they had slaughtered so many of the attackers.

Before the blockade began some of the richer women were put on one of the Earl of Warwick's Parliament ships to save them. But the ordinary women of Lyme were left to have their houses burned and be blown apart by grenadoes and fire arrows. These brave women shared every danger with their men, re-arming them, acting as look outs, cooking and caring for the wounded and in one poor woman's case getting killed whilst hanging out the laundry, another had her hand blown off by accidentally catching a grenadoe as she did not know what it was.

On the 14th June the seige ended and the Royalists left, then 400 women of the town flattened Prince Maurices earthworks and fortifications with spades and shovels and destroyed them completely in a week. It was the seige of Lyme that inspired the following poem by James Strong.

"To most tis known,The weaker vessels are the stronger grown. The vine on which the pole still lean'd his arms Must now bear up and save the pole from Harms."

Gloucester 1644: Quote from a pamphlet collected by John Dorney, the Town Clerk at the time:

"With cheerful readiness of young and old of both sexes to labour in the further fortification of our great city."

Young women who helped to build the earthworks worked daily until they were finished, then went out to gather fuel to cook their evening meal right in the face of the enemy.

So the war rolled on, battle after battle, father against son, mother against daughter, with women struggling to come to terms with not just the loss of their children by natural forces, but with the loss of their grown children to the Musket or the Halberd.

With men away fighting, women came into their own. Some remained quiet obedient wives and daughters and lived their lives as best they could. Others took to the musket and the sword, yet more defending what they had worked and strived for all their lives.

Sarah Evans of Chastleton House

Sarah Evans(Eyans) 1658 (xxv)

Sarah Evans was thirty five when this portrait was painted and she had just given birth to the last of the twelve children she was to bear her husband "The Cavalier" Arthur Jones.

They lived in Chastleton, a majestic honey coloured house on the borders of four counties Oxfordshire, Gloucestershire, Warwickshire and Worcestershire. Their house was beautifully appointed with the latest in stylish wall hangings, glassware, plate and furniture.

The Jones' were Royalists and then became Jacobites, rapidly losing their wealth as they were never on the winning side.

In the late 1940s whilst showing visitors round the house Sarah's descendant Irene Whitmore-Jones was still telling visitors that the family lost all it's money in the war - she didn't mean World War II- but the English Civil Wars of 300 years ago.

In 1651 seven years earlier than her portrait, Sarah was at home with her children whilst Arthur was fighting a losing battle at Worcester. He had joined forces with the Scots led by Charles II against Oliver Cromwell's Commonwealth Soldiers. The last battle of the Civil Wars was a defeat for the Royalist Armies, some of them escaped from the horror of the battlefield, Sarah's husband amongst them.

Arthur Jones of Chastleton House (xxvi)

Arthur arrived home exhausted and it was obvious to him that he'd been followed. The Roundheads were not far behind, so Sarah helped him hide in the secret room adjoining their bedchamber. She must have been beside herself with worry when Cromwell's men burst into her house demanding food and drink, while they waited for her husband to appear.

The hidden room with door open, when the door is closed the tapestry completely obscures the entrance and it looks just like a wall. The carpet is upturned because my husband tripped over it taking photos! (xxvii)

Sarah must have been horrified when the room the soldiers chose as their billet was her bedroom, probably because it was the best room in the house. Unknown to them, behind the hidden door her poor husband Arthur was hiding.

Keeping her wits about her she gave Cromwell's men a large flagon of ale laced with Laudanum, (about 1% opium and used as a painkiller in the 1600s) from the medicine chest. As soon as the soldiers fell into a deep drugged slumber she and Arthur must have crept over the bodies on the floor, holding their breath, out through their room and down to the stables.

Arthur borrowed one of the soldiers horses and made his getaway. It was two years before he felt it was safe enough for him to return home.

Chastleton House today is still magnificent,but fragile,crumbling away gently in the arms of the National Trust. The gardens are now full of the fruit that Sarah, Arthur and their children would have had on their tables. Medlars, peaches, apples,and pears grow alongside medicinal herbs in the well kept gardens.

Jane Lane: King's Rescuer

Whilst Sarah Evans was busy poisoning Commonwealth Soldiers with Laudenum, another audacious escape was taking place with the help of a woman.

After the Battle of Worcester in 1651, Charles II escaped and his journey led him to Boscobel House owned by the Catholic Penderel family. It was here that Charles II hid in the oak tree whilst Parliamentary soldiers searched for him, later he was hidden in the priest hole in the house.

The soldiers were looking for a "tall black man", the description of his hair colour in the common parlance. The King was six foot two, noticeably tall amongst an average height of five foot eight for men. There was a price of £1000 on the King's head and anyone helping him would be executed for treason if they were caught. One man, the servant of Charles Gifford a cousin of the Penderals, was executed for his part in the escape.

Jane Lane comes into the story when the King and his entourage arrived at the home of Colonel John Lane, her brother who had been an officer in the Royalist Army since 1642. One of Charles' party, Lord Wilmot, learned that Jane had obtained a permit from the military for herself and a servant to travel to Bristol to visit a relation, Ellen Norton, who was having a baby.

Lord Wilmot had the idea of the King escaping to Bristol disguised as her servant, as no lady of quality travelled alone. The King could make use of her military pass and travel to Bristol as Jane Lane's manservant. Once he was there he might find a ship to take him to France.

On the 10th of September 1651, Charles took on the identity of 'William Jackson' a tenant farmer's son. Dressed in the rough clothes of a farm labourer with his hair cut, the King left for Bristol. For his lady's protection 'William Jackson' rode the same horse as Jane Lane. Jane's sister, Withy Petre, her husband John Petre, with the Royalist Officer Henry Lascelles made up the party.

Lord Wilmot rode ahead of them pretending to be hunting, but looking out for trouble and distracting attention from his King.

By the time the party reached Bromsgrove, Jane and William's horse had shed a shoe and they needed to go to a blacksmith. It was William's job to take the horse to be shod.
Let's hear Charles tell the story :-

> *"As I was holding my horse's foot, I asked the smith what news. He told me that there was no news that he knew of, since the good news of the beating the rogues of the Scots. I asked him whether there was none of the English taken that joined with the Scots, He answered he did not hear if that rogue, Charles Stuart, were taken; but some of the others, he said, were taken. I told him that if that rogue were taken, he deserved to be hanged more than all the rest, for bringing in the Scots. Upon which he said I spoke like an honest man; and so we parted."*

I bet Charles was laughing as soon as he was out of sight. They stayed the night at a relation of Jane's, riding through Parliamentarian troops to get there.

The journey must have seemed lengthy and terrifying to Jane, but she kept a cool head as they passed through Stratford-upon-Avon to Cirencester and from there to Chipping Sodbury and finally Bristol. They had been riding through enemy territory for two days arriving on the 12th September at Jane's friends' home, the real reason for her visit, to see the pregnant Ellen Norton and her husband George, who did not realise they had Royalty staying under their roof.

William asked a fellow servant if he had ever seen the King, he looked at him and said, "Yes, he was taller than you!"

For all of Charles' good humour, Jane must have been relieved that her part in his escape was over. Unfortunately Jane's friend Ellen miscarried and wanted Jane to stay with her. Jane pretended that she had been called back to her home so she could leave with the King. There was no ship in Bristol to take him, so the next plan was to go to Lyme or Weymouth and try his luck there. Jane left Charles at Trent in Dorset to return home, leaving him to wait for his ship.

On 14th October Jane found out that the Council of State knew she had helped with the King's escape. Secretly before she could be arrested, Jane left Bentley Hall. This time it was she who was in disguise, as a simple country maid. She walked to Yarmouth and managed to get across to France, arriving in Paris in December 1651.

The Court in exile made her welcome and she became good friends with the King and his mother Queen Henrietta Maria. The King thought so much of his *plain Jane, that John Fisher reported a scurrillous rumour that she was the King's mistress. The King's sister, Mary, in a letter from Holland jokingly called Jane the King's 'wife'.

In 1652, Charles arranged for Jane to become a lady-in-waiting for his sister Princess Mary. During his time in France, Charles corresponded with Jane Lane and often said that he wished he could help her more, he was obviously very fond of her.

Here is a letter from Charles to Jane in reply to a letter she had sent him saying he must have forgotten her:

1652 the last of June

Mrs. Lane, I did not thinke I should ever have begun a letter to you in chiding, but you give me so just cause by telling me you feare you are wearing out of my memory that I cannot chuse but tell you I take it very unkindly that after all the obligations I have to you 'tis possible for you to suspect I can ever be so wanting to myselfe as not to remember them on all occasions to your advantage?, which I assure you, I shall and hope before long I shall have it in my power to give you testimonyes of my kindnesse to you which I desire. I am very sorry to hear that your father and brother are in prison, but I hope it is of no other score than the general claping of all persons who wish me well and I am the more sorry for it. Now it hath hindered you from coming along with my sister that I might have assured you myself how truly I am

Your Most affectionate friend,

Jane returned to England when the King was restored to his throne. Charles gave her a pension of £1000 per year, portraits of himself, and a lock of his hair. He was grateful to the woman who put her life at risk for him just by letting him become her servant. She was also given £1000 by Parliament to buy a jewel to commemorate her service to the King, and the right to add the Three Lions of England to her coat of arms to bear witness to her exceptional courage and faithfulness to the Crown.

On the 8th December 1663 she was married to Sir Clement Fisher, 2nd Baronet of Great Packington. Fisher had served under Jane's brother, John Lane, in the First Civil War, and this was probably how he was introduced to Jane. Lady Fisher had no children, but she did have expensive tastes, at one time £6500 in debt because of her extravagant lifestyle. She died at the age of 63 at Packington Old Hall leaving a life well lived and an estate worth £10. She is buried at Packington.

Note **Isn't it amazing how women being called "Plain Jane" over the years didn't realise that the woman who probably started this insult,rescued a King who probably loved her,and went on to become a great Lady. To see a portrait of Jane go to Jane's home, National Trust owned Moseley Old Hall, and judge for yourself.*

Mary Frith the Roaring Girl

(xxviii)

I first heard about Moll Cutpurse when I lived in the centre of London. She was more recently brought to back to my mind when the Sealed Knot helped to open the Civil War Centre in Newark. In the shop were canvas bags bearing her name and a drawing of her at work.

When I lived in London, her skill of relieving men of their purses, in such a way that gave them pleasure that they allowed it. was the stuff of legend.

Moll was born Mary in 1584 in the Barbican in London, not far from where I used to live. Her parents Ron and Catherine owned a shoemakers shop.

She was a handful as a child, a tomboy, always getting into trouble of some sort or another. Her father's brother was a minister and suggested they send the girl to the New World, hoping that would calm her down and give her the adventure she craved.

But Mary was having none of it, she left the ship before it sailed and began her life of crime in London. She dressed as a boy and because of her outrageous behaviour, stealing, smoking and swearing in public, she quickly became notorious.

She took various names. Moll was a generic name for a woman, like Sheila in Australia today, she also called herself Mal Cutpurse and Tom Falconer. She was called a “Roaring Girl” because young men of the day who drank in taverns and caused fights were “Roaring Boys”, today we'd call them yobs.

She always seemed to dress like a man, to give herself more freedom to do what she wanted. Cross-dressing in the 17thC was lewd behaviour, but this didn't seem to bother her. She had the palm of her hands burned four times as the mark of a thief, but she never obeyed the law if she could help it.

It was said of her :-
“She could not endure the sedentary life of sewing and stitching, a sampler was as grievous to her as a winding sheet.”

She was a bully and a thug, she lived in Fleet Street when she wasn't in Newgate Prison, and employed a gang of thieves and maids to look after her house. She kept expensive pets, parrots and dogs which she took great care of, it's said her house was full of mirrors as she was very vain.

Moll became somewhat of a celebrity and had a comedy written about her by Thomas Middleton and Thomas Dekker. Even taking to the stage herself at the Fortune theatre to sing lewd songs dressed as a man, accompanying herself on a lute.

William Banks, who also wrote a play about her, bet her £20 pounds that she couldn’t ride from Charing Cross to Shoreditch dressed as a man. As she always dressed as a man it wasn't a problem, but Moll being Moll, did it on Banks' own horse, one of the first performing horses in England, blowing a trumpet and waving a flag. I imagine it was one of the easiest £20 she had ever earned.

She married Lewknor Markham, the son of the famous writer Gervais Markham in 1614 as she did not particularly care for being called a spinster when summoned to court. The wedding was false as the only interest that Moll had in sex was running her ring of prostitutes.

The Civil War did encroach on Moll's life when she made the mistake of robbing Cromwell's General Fairfax and shooting him in the arm, she seemed to claim insanity for the act and after a spell in Bedlam she was released in June 1644.

However a stay in Newgate prison followed and as the gallows beckoned Moll paid a £2000 bribe to escape the hangman's noose, a considerable amount. In todays money it would be worth about £86k.

Nothing changed Moll's way of life and after the Civil War she became one of the first highwaywoman. She still had spells in Newgate this time as a visitor to feed the prisoners from her huge wealth. She died of dropsy in the summer of 1659 aged 75 after a long and exciting life robbing the rich and giving to the poor (herself!).

The Baggage Trayne

Sealed Knot re-enactment where Women are acting as the Baggage train (xxix)

The women of the Baggage train have always had a raw deal, even today in the Sealed Knot I think that the usefulness of the Baggage is under-rated. There are still some who do not want to see women in skirts on the field, let alone with cooking utensils, and children on the wagons, but in accompanying the army in real life 17th century warfare that was exactly how they travelled.

If it wasn't for the 17thC women of the Baggage train and their armed guards, the troops would not have come off the field of war to the comfort of their wives and lovers, or had their wounds dressed with salves and clean bandages, or fed hot provinder. The Baggage train was guarded because it provided gold to pay the troops, shot, black powder, spare weapons and of course food. There would be a blacksmith who could shoe horses, an armourer, a jack of all trades who could mend anything who had possibly been a tinker before the war. There may also have been a doctor and a midwife amongst the Baggage train. Sometimes women of quality, the high ranking officer's wives, would travel in coaches behind the Baggage to be with their husbands as they went to war.

Never was the Baggage so abused than at Naseby Battlefield. Around 12,000 soldiers were on the field that day, Cromwell and Fairfax had won the battle with about 4000 infantry surrendering. The cavalry had galloped off with the Kings Lifeguard running behind them as if their lives depended on it, which of course they did.

What was left on Naseby Battlefield was the Royal Artillery train with it's powder, 8000 weapons and the colours (the identifying flags). Leaving behind the Baggage train with the women and children. Their armed guards having run off to fight another day. What followed was unadulterated plunder, rape and slaughter.
To quote Lord Clarendon:

> *"The enemy left no manner of barbarous cruelty unexercised that day and in the pursuit killed above one hundred women,whereof some were officers' wives of quality."*

Some of the officers' wives managed to buy their freedom with their jewels and clothing, but many the soldier's wives and the camp followers were slaughtered mercilessly. Many women had their noses slit before they were murdered - marking them out as prostitutes.

Over a hundred women died that day, hacked to pieces because it was thought they were Irish. Prince Rupert made an abortive attempt to help the the Baggage, but was driven off by the weight of Parliament troops advancing towards him so he galloped away to join the King. Over one hundred thousand pounds in gold, silver and jewels were taken, as well as the Kings personal correspondence.

Naseby today is a quiet field in Northamptonshire used as a training ground by the Sealed Knot. They are hoping to buy it and save it from becoming a housing estate.

Prince Ruperts Bluecoats famously made their last stand there, fighting to the last man, they are buried under a mound in a field up the road. There is nothing that marks the women's sacrifice, or denotes where they died.

The women re-enacting the Baggage today are basically doing the same as their 17th century counterparts, although now it's called Health and Safety.

They give water to the troops, attend to the wounded sometimes there are wounded as accidents do happen. Soldiers overheat and faint, get crushed in the pike pushes or need to be helped to get to the Medics tent.

They also need on the field maintenance when they break the straps of their helmets, shoes or armour, or need someone to take a broken pike or sword back to camp. They need rehydrate tablets on a very hot day, the Baggage women today carry huge amounts of water in the wicker baskets on their backs and leather sacks over their arms. They do a wonderful job, they also provide a visual reminder to the public of what the soldiers were fighting for. Their families and their homes.

However, I feel that women are like chaff in the wind. Their bodies and souls blow away without leaving a mark, which is one of the reasons I am writing this book. For them.

Lady Brilliana Harley

(xxx)

Brilliana was born in Brill near Rotterdam, Holland in 1598. Her enterprising parents, the Conways, must have thought it appropriate to name her after her birthplace where her father Sir Edward Conway was serving as Governor. (see chapter on Puritan names)

Brilliana was brought up in Holland for part of her young life, as the well educated daughter of a staunchly Puritan family. The family returned to England in 1606, where she became a pious, if radical, religious young woman. She was married late, probably because Sir Edward had problems raising the dowries needed, as the father of three daughters it would have been a tidy sum to find even for a successful Parliamentarian.

When she was 25 she became the third wife of Sir Robert Harley, who was her father's aide in parliament, when he became the Secretary of State for England. Sir Robert was in his forties and badly wanted a son and heir. His previous wives had provided daughters and then died.

They made their home at Brampton Bryan Castle in Herefordshire where Brilliana provided Robert with a son every two years from the time of her marriage to him in 1623 until 1628, Edward, Robert and Thomas. She then topped her success off with four daughters, Brilliana, Dorothy, and Margaret. Unfortunately the youngest daughter Elizabeth was the only one of the children not to survive.

It was a happy marriage, both Puritans with the same mindset, they had made a strong bond between them. But during the Civil War they were often apart, and this is where Brilliana's story really starts.

Brilliana was already used to being amongst her enemies. Ludlow, her nearest town, and Brampton were Royalist, and quite often she would hear the townspeople insult her as they passed by. To use her own words in a letter to her husband:

"they are grown exceeding rude in these parts. Every Thursday some of Ludlow as they go through Brampton wish all the Puritans of Brampton hanged, they looked upon me and cursed you and all your children, as they do every week."

Unsurprisingly Brilliana did not feel safe in her own home, and wrote to Robert asking if she could bring the children and come and be with him in London. His reply was also unsurprising. No.

He thought leaving the house empty would give the local Royalists an opportunity to loot and destroy his family home. He may have also thought that with the plague rife in London, the countryside was a better place to be for his wife and children.

Brilliana wrote back and said:

"If you think Brampton is safe, then I will think so too. I would not do anything that might make the world believe our hopes did begin to fail in God."

She wrote to her son Ned who was old enough to be in London with his father, that she would not leave everything his father has to the prey of his enemies, and thanked God she was not afraid.

Her son Ned became her close friend. She wrote to Ned more often than his father, and told him about life at home, and how she missed him. In her short life Brilliana wrote over 350 letters, some of which survive today.

At home things were getting worse, Brilliana's tenants were no longer paying their rents and their hate against her husband was growing every day. In July along with buying provinder, she found herself buying Muskets, Bandoliers and shot secretly, and writing to her husband to ask the best way to have the house guarded.

Since the rents were not being paid, money was also starting to become a problem and many of the local workmen wanted to charge exorbitant prices for their work for repairs to the house, either to price themselves out of a job or make money out of their enemies.
In December 1642 Brilliana wrote to her son Ned:

> *"My heart has had no rest since you left, I confess I was never so full of sorrow. I fear the provision of corn and malt will not hold out, if this continue; and they burn my barns; my fear is that they will place soldiers so much near me that there will be no going out. My comfort is that you are not with me, lest they should take you, but I do most dearly miss you. I wish, if it had pleased God, that I were with your father. I would have written him, but I durst not write upon paper. Dear Ned write to me, though write on a piece of cloth as this is. I pray God bless you, as I desire my own soul to be blessed."*

Note: Cloth could be folded and hidden in clothing which was why Brilliana suggested it to her son.

In January 1643 Fitzwilliam Coningsby was ordered to attack Brampton. As the Royalists moved in, one of her servants, called Griffiths, was arrested and "cruelly used". She could do nothing to help him. Her food supplies were being cut off, her horses were driven away, and her servants were too frightened to go into the town. She had heard that around 600 soldiers were heading to Brampton Bryan.

Brilliana was working against the clock, time was moving on and in February she had the moat filled with water. Hereford, which had been in the hands of Parliament, had been taken by the Royalists. They were getting closer to Brampton. Most of the local men were joining the army on one side or the other, she couldn't let her own men go as she was afraid the house would be attacked and looted.

Luckily the invading forces were called away to the Forest of Dean and Brilliana thanked God for the respite, even though she had been threatened with being starved out with the loss of her cattle.

Then she received a summons demanding that she hand over her house or punished as a traitor.

"It may be everyone's case to be made traitors, for believe everyone will be as unwilling to part with their house as I am."

Strangely, Brilliana kept up with the news and heard that Lathom House, held by Lady Charlotte Derby, had not fallen. All Lancashire is cleared, she said pleased at the triumph, "Except Lathom House." She was disappointed by this, she didn't seem to link Lady Derby's fate to that of her own.

Then came more arrests, Samuel More who was at Brampton was taken. In May she lost her faithful servant Honest Petter, six men set upon him and shot him three times. He fought them and managed to injure two, but he didn't stand a chance at six to one and ended up wounded and in Ludlow prison. Also that month saw her beloved son Ned and his brother Robin join Waller's regiment, and the regiment of Herefordshire Cavaliers return to Brampton.

On the 25th of July the Siege of Brampton Bryan began in earnest. The Royalist Commander William Vavasour made a concerted attempt to raze Brampton Bryan to the ground. Driving off the remaining cattle and eating them, burning the farm buildings, and keeping up a constant barrage of cannon and musket fire.

Brilliana's teenage children, Thomas, Dorothy and Margaret were in the castle during the six weeks that the siege lasted, but still she would not surrender. The cook was shot dead, two other servants wounded. The castle so damaged that no room was warm or dry.

By September, Brilliana was still refusing to surrender, certain her home would be destroyed as soon as she left it. There was a small respite when the army were called away to attack Essex's army in Gloucester. As soon as they were gone, Brilliana directed her servants to level the earthworks the Royalists had built. She also managed to send 40 troops to raid the Royalist camp at Knighton. But these were little victories.

October brought bad news, Brilliana and Brampton were again threatened. Sir William Vavasour had returned with re-enforcements just as she felt herself going down with a cold. She wrote:
"I have taken a very great cold, which has made me very ill these 2 or 3 days, but I hope the Lord will be merciful to me in giving me my health, for it is an ill time to be sick in."
Her cold had turned to flu and her husband Sir Robert was given a letter on the 29th October by one of his servants to tell him that Brilliana was seriously ill, suffering from a bad flu complicated by exhaustion and stress. Her servant, Samuel More, could see she was dying and sent for her son Ned to come and be at her side. Brilliana died as she lived - bravely and calmly on 31st October 1643 aged 45.

Charlotte Stanley, Countess of Derby

(xxxi)

Charlotte was born in Poitou in France in 1599, the daughter of a French nobleman Claude de la Tremoille, Duke of Thours and his wife Charlotte Brabantina of Nassau. Descendant of a long line of distinguished noblemen and women, the nearest thing you could get to Royalty without being one.

She came to England, because her mother accompanied Henrietta-Maria to her marriage to King Charles. Her mother arranged another marriage, that of her daughter Charlotte, to James Stanley, 7th Earl of Derby and Lord of the Isle of Man, which took place in the Hague in July 1626.

The Stanleys lived in the style of the minor Royals they were at Lathom House in Lancashire, employing over two hundred servants. Although Lord

Stanley was tall, dark, and handsome, he was also vain, arrogant, self-centred and bad tempered.

Charlotte was pleased with Lathom and the young Lord (19 when they married) that she wrote to thank her mother for settling her so comfortably.

After being married for a year Charlotte was still happy, saying her husband showed her great affection. In January 1628 Charlotte gave birth to her first child, a son called Charles. He was christened dressed in white; the French style, in the chapel at Lathom, by the Bishop of Chester.

Charlotte was a single-minded woman, and caused chaos when she forbade the baby to be swaddled, and worse of all allowed her son to suck his thumb!

The Stanleys were committed Royalists but despite his lofty birth, James held no particular office in the Court.

The English Civil War broke out at about the same time as James succeeded to his father's title, so the new Earl of Derby went off to fight. His attack on the town of Manchester, with his private army, ended in failure. In 1643 they turned their attention to Lancaster and Preston, sacking, plundering and burning as they went. They were routed by a few hundred musketeers at Sabden Brook some thirty miles from Lathom. This effectively put an end to his military command and made him decide to visit his other lands in the Isle of Man to sort out long standing land tenure problems. What James Stanley had effectively done was to make Lancashire an important Parliamentarian base and bring the Royalist cause into disrepute.

Almost as soon as Lord Derby had set foot on his ship to the Isle of Man, Charlotte Derby received a summons to turn to Parliament or yield up Lathom House. She was prepared to do neither. But Lathom was now surrounded since Parliament had taken back Preston and occupied Warrington.

There would be no Royalist help coming any time soon so Lady Derby offered a compromise. She would give up the estate lands to Parliament and made a promise to keep only as many men at arms to defend herself and her household from the ravages of the common soldiers.

She had bought herself some time, but when she walked close to the house in the gardens with her two young daughters Mary and Catherine, she, like Brilliana Harley, was insulted and barracked by the local people.

"She patiently endured, well knoweing it no wisdome to quarrell with an evil she could not redresse."

Taken from a Briefe Journall of the Siege against Lathom.

What Charlotte was doing was using the time to collect men, arms and money before the awaited attack on Lathom began. She also went out of her way not to offend the enemy in case they realised what she was up to.

On the weekend of 24/25th February 1644 Charlotte received secret information that parliament forces were marching on Lathom House. On the 27th February Thomas Fairfax (known as Black Tom) took up positions about two miles away from Lathom. He sent a letter to Charlotte requesting she "yield up" Lathom House. She replied that she needed a week to think about it and give her answer for as far as she was concerned she had done nothing wrong.

Thomas Fairfax knew she was trying to buy time so he suggested that they meet to discuss the matter. Her Ladyship could take her coach to a house nearby where they could sit down and talk about it. Her reply was curt. Roughly translated from the Early Modern English,

"Remember who I am, it is not for me to wait upon you, it is more knightly for you to wait upon me as you are of lower birth."

There followed a heated exchange of letters, but on the 2nd of March Charlotte allowed two of Fairfax's men into Lathom bearing the terms of surrender.

They were:

Immediate surrender of the House with all it's arms and ammunition.

The garrison could leave with their possessions.

> The Countess could go to Knowsley, the Derby's hunting lodge, with twenty musketeers, or she may join her husband on the Isle of Man.

If she agreed, Parliament would allow her to keep the Earl's revenues for her maintenance.

The answer was no, she wanted to stay where she was. As far as she was concerned the offer was dishonourable and uncertain. Charlotte wanted to make her own proposals, so on the following Monday Captain Ashton returned to hear what she had to say:

> A month in quiet continuence at Lathom to prepare to leave.
> Free transport to the Isle of Man for herself and her children, all her friends and her household.
> The garrison to stay where it was but the arms were not to be used against Parliament.
> None of her neighbours or tenants who supported her should suffer in any way after she left.

Captain Ashton left knowing that her demands were only intended to buy Lathom more time. They couldn't be met, they were too full of policy and danger. It was clear that Lady Charlotte Derby did not recognise Parliament as a force to be reckoned with.

Fairfax tried again, this time sending Colonel Morgan. The Countess could have a month to pack then transport her arms and goods to the Isle of Man. She must leave her cannon. Her garrison must however be disbanded by 10 o'clock the following day, and she was to agree to accept a guard of forty Parliament soldiers.

She refused, and realising she could "scrue them to no more delays" told them she'd rather die than negotiate with them again, and though a woman and a stranger in this country, robbed of her estate, she was ready to fight, and she was going to defend her home for her Church, her Prince and her husband, and trust in God for deliverance.

The Parliamentarians moved quickly into the park nearer the house and started to dig a line of trenches within musket range.

Lathom's garrison consisted of 300 well trained soldiers, the house itself had high thick walls and was built on rising ground on three sides, almost impossible to beseige.

The Parliamentarians were hoping to starve the garrison out, believing it could only have provisions for a couple of weeks. Fairfax was hoping that the Countess would come to terms when the supplies ran out. They were unaware that there was a secret tunnel from the Castle to the town, so supplies would not be a problem as the servants could come and go as usual.

On the 10th of March a group of the local gentry of the highest rank took a petition to Charlotte to ask her to consider the danger she was in. They were worried that their livelihoods and lands would be destroyed as well if there was a full attack on Lathom. Charlotte replied that the petitioners would be better off talking to Parliament, they were the ones who robbed and spoiled the countryside, not her. All she wanted was a quiet stay in her own house. They left.

On the 11th Captain Ashton returned. Thomas Fairfax wanted them all out, today, free to take their possessions and arms (which were not to be used against Parliament) and go where they please, except a rearguard of 100 people who must leave within ten days.

Charlotte distrusted the offer, how could she bargain if the sword was in the enemies hand? In brief, she wanted no more messages unless they came from her husband who she had heard had just returned from the Isle of Man. She was keeping her house.

James, Earl of Derby had in fact returned, he'd been back a while, spending time with the King in Oxford. He had already written to Fairfax asking for free passage for his wife and daughters, he was not sure how they would cope if it came to a seige.

Charlotte was not one to give up, she managed to send a full report of the situation at Lathom to the Earl by a messenger.

The beseigers had not fired one shot at Lathom. Captain Farmer, who was in command of the garrison at Lathom, obviously thought the best form of defence was to attack. To this end he led a hundred foot soldiers and the entire Lathom cavalry to attack the Parliamentarians in their trenches. They killed thirty and took six prisoners.

About a week later the commanders, under her Ladyship, tested the enemy night watch. Captain Chisenhall, two officers and thirty musketeers crept out of the back gate and surprised them, this time killing two or three and chasing the rest into the woods.

There were around two or three thousand Parliamentarian troops taking it in turns to be on duty. Taking their food and pay from the towns around Lathom, with soldiers billeted in any houses that could accomodate them. It was turning out to be a very expensive endeavour for the county.

Thomas Fairfax was needed in Yorkshire so he left Lathom around the end of March leaving Colonel Alexander Rigby in charge. He wasn't really a military man, although he started bombardment of Lathom around the 20th of March, it was badly done and had little effect.

He wasted enormous amounts of shot and powder pounding the walls. Part of the tower was damaged and two defenders killed, but that was the sum total of their efforts. A new seige machine was brought forward, a large mortar that could fire grenadoes (early grenades that exploded on contact) and huge stone balls weighing around 80 pounds. These would be launched into the air to land inside the castle walls to set fire to the wood and thatch interior. The household were waiting with buckets of water and wet hides to quench the flames, they needn't have bothered. Both missiles missed!

Strangely in the middle of this battle the Puritans decided to hold a four day prayer meeting. It was an unexpected respite that Captains Farmer and Radcliffe took advantage of. They led half the garrison out of the postern gate, threw the enemy off their batteries which now surrounded the house, sabotaged their cannons, killed 50 men, took 60 arms (muskets or swords), one set of colours (the honour of the regiment), and their drums. Drums were important, their beats conveyed messages such as advance or retreat.

Captain Radcliffe alone killed 7 men, his troop being scattered. Captain Chisenhall was waiting at the front gates of Lathom in case his re-inforcements were needed. One enemy officer was taken for intelligence and only one Lathom man was badly wounded. Charlotte did not want such carnage, but the garrison had no more room for prisoners.

It was a short lived victory though and the bombardment started again with a vengence, one musket ball entering Lady Derby's bedroom, but it was the mortar that was doing the real damage. Luckily no-one was hurt, two maids near the chamber where a grenadoe fell had their hands burnt trying to put it out, "to putt them in mind herafter that they were in the seige at Lathom."

The main aim of the garrison now became to destroy the mortar piece. One of it's engineers was killed by one of Lady Derby's snipers. The Lathom snipers were known for their deadly accuracy, all former gamekeepers and fowlers employed on the estate and they hardly ever missed.

The seige had now lasted for a whole two months and the Parliamentarians were getting exhausted. They were on constant watch, with regular alarms throughout the night, they were getting very little sleep. Colonel Rigby complained that he was "spent with anxiety and fatigue." He made the mistake of trying to bully the Countess into submission, on 25th April he sent what he called a "furious summons" to tell her to get everybody and all her goods and possessions out of the house, it would be her last chance to surrender.

Charlotte received the message sitting amongst the captains and officers of her garrison. For a moment she considered hanging the messenger, but she needed him to take her reply back to Colonel Rigby. It would not be an easy message to deliver.

She called Rigby insolent for even suggesting such a thing. No one was going to get their hands on her people, goods or house. She said she would rather burn the house down as it stood; soldiers, herself and her children, rather than let it fall into Rigby's hands. At this her household cheered and shouted "We'll dye for his Majesty and your Honour."

As things were as bad as they could get, the Countess and her captains sat together to decide what they should do next. What they decided was to throw caution to the wind and try to take out the mortar, it was the piece of armoury that everyone in Lathom feared most.

On April 26th, as dawn broke on a wet spring morning, Captain Chisenhall and a party of men slipped out of the castle and surprised the half-asleep and cold enemy in their trenches. They fiercely fought their way towards the mortar on the great earthworks, advancing through musket and cannon fire to climb over the top. Many of the Parliamentarians ran for their lives, but many others were killed.

During the fighting the Parliamentarians attempted to take the mortar emplacment back, but were held off by a squadron of Lathom musketeers. With re-inforcements from Lathom they roped the mortar to a sledge and dragged it back to the House. It took about an hour, but everyone was pleased with what they had achieved.

Later that day, Colonel Rigby returned to Lathom with his friends to share with them the excitment of the grenadoes and fireballs burning Latham to the ground. Instead he must have felt embarrassed, as his friends saw that he had been outwitted by a middle aged portly matron with a handful of musketeers and soldiers!

Inside Lathom there was celebrations as the monster lay in their yard. Many gave it a kick as they drank beer, played their bagpipes and danced round it. Charlotte who had not showed much emotion through the seige, apart from anger, was extremely pleased and did not hide it. She asked the Chaplains to give a special service of thanksgiving for their victory.

Parliamentarian soldiers tried to drain the moat but heavy rain caused an avalanche of mud that killed three men. They were being constantly harried by the Lathom Garrison who gave them no rest, attacking at random times during the night. They even moved their gun emplacements out of the way of those “mad men” in the Castle.

Meanwhile Lord Derby was trying to get help for his wife and children, as the Countess refused yet another summons from Colonel Rigby to surrender. On the 27th of May, a humiliated Colonel Rigby, on hearing that Prince Rupert and re-inforcements were heading for Lathom, packed up and left. The siege of Lathom was over.

Part of Lathom House as it is today. (xxxii)

Countess Charlotte, died at Knowsley in March 1644, aged 65. Throughout her adventurous life keeping to her family mottos "I maintain" and "Without Change."

Basing House - Aymez Loyalte

Basing House by Wenceslaus Hollar (xxxiii)

The Sealed Knot re-enactments at Basing House are usually towards the start of of the season, everyone is raring to go. Nantwich on Holly Holy Day around the 22nd of January seems an age away, and come the first May Bank Holiday at Basing House everyone is ready to go fight for the King or Parliament.

I usually walk round the ruins of Basing the day before, trying to imagine what it would have been like waiting for the enemy to come. Basing was a crown jewel, a mixture of a Tudor motte and bailey castle and 17th century family house linked by a bridge. Basing was renowned throughout the country for it's richness and luxury.

I currently work at Waddesdon Manor, although Victorian, the owner Ferdinand de Rotheschild collected and preserved 17th Century French furniture, it still glitters, the tapestries now faded, still warm the walls. Some 16th Century carpets survive full of flock and colour almost looking new. I often wonder if this was what Basing looked like before Colonel Dalbier and Cromwell pounded it into rubble.

At the time of the outbreak of the English Civil War in 1642, Basing House belonged to John Paulet the fifth Marquis of Winchester. He was a devout Catholic who was a supporter of King Charles. The magnificent Basing House was fit for Royalty, a palace in all but name.

The Marquis' wife, The Marchioness of Winchester, was born Lady Honora de Burgh, a half sister to the Earl of Essex. This put William Waller, the first Parliamentarian to attack Basing in a difficult position. The Earl of Essex was the Chief Commander of the Parliament army, so Waller could hardly order an attack on the Earl's sister.

William Waller decided to offer free passage to her Ladyship and all the women and children in Basing. The Marchioness refused saying:

"Whatever befel us I am not unprepared to bear it."

But it was Waller's men who had to bear it, it was bitterly cold on the 6th of November with driving rain that turned to snow. His men slept at night in the open fields around Basing. It wasn't long after being driven off from their first assault, the London Trayned Bands were begging to go back to their homes.

Waller decided to have another go at Basing trying to blow a hole in the wall of the earthworks. It did not work.

Another contingent of his men managed to get into Basing Park, but coming close under the walls, found themselves being attacked by women throwing slates off the roof and stones and bricks, injuring the men. Waller lost around 250 men in the three days he attacked the house, some by musket shot and some by "friendly fire" they turned in their ranks to reload and started shooting before the second rank retired, killing and wounding many of their own men.

Probably used as an excuse for deserters, when a Robert Rodway was killed in this stupid accident, a letter from his wife was found in his belongings. Her private pleas for him to come home were publicised, calling her an insolent women, and blaming her for cries of "Home Home" from the troops.
Her letter is as follows:

Most Dear and loving Husband,my King Love,remember unto you hoping you are in good health as I am at the writing hereof. My little Willie has been sick this fortnight. I pray you to come home if you can come safely. I do marvel that I cannot hear from you as well as other neighbours do. I do desire to hear from you as soon as you can. I pray you send me word when you think you shall return.You do not consider I am a lone woman. I thought you would never leave me this long together. I rest ever praying for your safe return, Your loving wife Susan Rodway, ever praying for you till death I depart.

It seems that poor Susan paid for the love of her husband by being ridiculed for wanting him home. But the seige of Basing continued, with the Marchioness and her ladies making musket balls with the lead from the roofs. The Marchioness managed to get out of Basing after Waller called off the attack because he had a shortage of ammunition. She made her way to Oxford to get arms and re-inforcements. However, Oxford's Governor Sir Arthur Aston, refused to help, saying Basing was 40 miles away and if his men did manage to get there, they may not get back.

It was about this time that the Marchioness received a desperate message from her husband, he could only hold out for ten days at the most. Luckily for Honora, an experienced professional soldier had just arrived in Oxford. Henry Gage arrived with a troop of Gentleman Volunteers and offered to help, he was joined by a small group of Hawkins Regiment, and this small force of arms left Oxford for Basing on 9th September, carrying powder and match through the back lanes for 36 hours disguised as Parliamentarians.

Henry Gage fought his way through the Parliament lines to Basing House, left his reinforcements of 100 musketeers to help with the defence, and promptly went shopping in Basingstoke, returning with about 50 cows, 100 sheep, wheat, salt, oats, bacon and cheese. Colonel Gage had brought enough food for a month, he left with his troops, still disguised as Parliamentarians, to join the Oxford Army. Basing was saved - for the moment.

In August 1645 the Malignant Basing was under seige again by Colonel Jan Dalbier, a Dutch engineer. On the 8th he was joined by none other than Cromwell himself, both of them eager to see this Catholic house pounded into the ground. Cromwell had already called for The Marquis to surrender and had been refused.

Dalbier had an experienced eye and knew just where to put his munitions to do the most damage. The great tower fell on 22nd September, the cannon destroyed the Tudor House so totally that bedding and other household goods fell into the courtyard.

The Marchioness had left Basing House just before Cromwell's arrival, perhaps her brother told her that Old Noll was on his way and she should leave. Just as well, what happened next was unadulterated slaughter.

Cromwell had ordered no quarter to be given, so every man, woman and child would be killed. The Parliamentarians took prisoners to the Great Barn and shot them against the doors. The musket ball holes are still there today. The women of the house were dragged out, stripped, raped, then murdered. Their fine dresses thrown to the troops as booty. Gentlewomen were apparently entertained in a coarse fashion by the common soldiers, they were left alive, with a few clothes still on them, they got off lightly considering the mayhem around them. The Catholic Priests hiding in the house were killed on the spot. Inigo Jones, the famous architect, an old man by then, was dragged onto the lawn and stripped naked. He was given a blanket to cover himself.

Women threw themselves in front of their men to save them, the daughter of Dr Griffiths tried to protect her father, calling the Parliamentarians - Roundheads and Rebels - an insult - and they dashed her brains out for her trouble. One poor man who was a famous comedian and clown from Drury Lane called Robinson, had been visiting Basing. He was shot trying to escape. This shows that the Parliamentarians had no sense of humour.

Although there was supposedly no quarter given, around 300 prisoners were taken, amongst them The Marquis of Winchester. He was taken to the House of Commons and then to the Tower of London. His offence? Taking up arms against Parliament to protect his family, home and belongings.

Suddenly it became all about the plunder and pillaging, although the rape and murder still went on all day. The Marquis was immensely wealthy with money, jewels, plate, and other riches. The people from the surrounding villages came with carts to help themselves. The London Trayned Bands helped themselves to the plate, hangings and works of art to sell on.

Cromwell was eager to move on. Prisoners and injured soldiers were put into the cellars. Hugh Peters, Cromwell's Chaplain, called them "unfortunates", they certainly were. An incendiary that had been smouldering away unnoticed in the murderous rampage burst into flames. The fire burnt all day and all night and by the following morning, nothing but the charred walls of the cellars were all that remained.

Despite hearing the cries and screams of the "unfortunates" Cromwell and Hugh Peters did nothing. Hugh Peters said they were unable to come out and their men couldn't go in.

My personal opinion is that they could have tried. Some of their own men were in there. I've walked in those cellars, and there is a strange peace about them nowadays. With the sun shining and the grass neatly mowed, Basing has become a romantic ruin. That night must have been hell for those men, and all that is left of their lives are black stains on the brickwork.

As for Honora she joined John in the Tower with her children. They were granted an allowance of £10 a week to live on, and it was later increased to £15 if they agreed to bring the children up in the Protestant faith. Like many other disenfranchised Royalists they were allowed leave to live abroad.

The beautiful palace that Wenceslaus Hollar drew was never rebuilt. It's riches no doubt turning up occasionally on the Antiques Roadshow, with the current owners having no idea how they came by them.

The Marquis and Marchioness of Winchester did return to England after the Restoration to live in retirement in Englefield House Berkshire and the ruins of Basing were returned to them.

I was puzzled by the rape,violence,slaughter and theft inflicted on the inhabitants of Basing by the Parliament Armies. Who prayed to God Almighty and sang hymns before every battle and had their preachers preach sermons to them. Weren't Christians supposed to be loving and kind?

I asked my husband what he thought. He just looked at me and said. “They were men,and that's what men do when they're at war.”

Lady Mary Bankes

A courage above her sex (xxxiv)

In 1634 Sir John Bankes, his 36 year old wife Mary and their children, moved into Corfe Castle, a hilltop fortress in Dorset. John was a Yuppie of the day and was pleased with his latest investment which gave him a Castle on five acres of land good for raising sheep, and the financially lucrative Purbeck stone quarries.

Sir John was a very rich man and Mary must have enjoyed decorating the castle with the finest goods money could buy. Tapestries hung on the walls, the windows hung with silks and damasks with velvet cushions on the window seats. Turkey and Persian carpets covered the cold stone floors, the chairs were covered in red velvet to match the bedding and the bed curtains to keep out the drafts. It would be a warm, inviting home even in the winter.

One thing the castle was short of was cannon, the previous owner Lady Hatton had sold the largest of them, thinking they were no longer needed.

Where Mary was described as being prudent, her husband was described as being a dour, sensible lawyer. They had married in 1618 when Mary was 20, and John had a good future in front of him, becoming Charles' Ist's Attorney General. They were both intelligent people and when the war was on the horizon in 1642 John went to serve the King in York. Mary, her children and servants moved into Corfe on the eve of the start of the Civil War to wait the war out in a Castle which had never yet been taken by an enemy.

In her portrait Lady Mary Bankes holds the keys to Corfe Castle, which you can see painted in the distance behind her. Look at her eyes, the firm set of her jaw, the grip on the keys, this was her beautiful home and she was not going to give it up easily.

Of all the Seige Matrons, Lady Mary held out the longest, six months. She was prepared, she had been gathering a huge store of provisions and those keys in her hand kept the Castle doors locked at all times. Unfortunately, to begin with, her garrison only consisted of her maidservants, five soldiers, and her daughters. Her sons had been sent away for safety as male heirs were often ransomed or killed.

The Parliamentarians must have had a very strange view of Lady Mary; believing she would be simple enough to be tricked into giving them the keys to her magnificent home without a fight.

On May Day, part of the festivities was for the Mayor and local Barons to take part in the ancient tradition of hunting a stag on Corfe land. The Parliamentarian troop of horse wanted to join in, but for a very different reason, they were hoping to take the Castle when everyone was distracted. Fortunately the Parliamentarian plan had been leaked, and when some of the troops from Dorchester tried to surprise Lady Bankes, she called in the guard. The Commanders of the troops denied the accusation. Lady Mary, like the other Seige Matrons, found herself being sworn at by common soldiers when they discovered that she was not as stupid as they were expecting her to be. Again, like Lady Derby and Brilliana Harley, she did not answer back, although sorely tempted. She was not quite prepared yet for the fight to come.

When the Poole Parliamentary Commitee of seamen tried to take the four small cannons left in the Castle, Lady Mary played for time. She checked their warrants, and then changed her mind about letting the seaman have her cannon. She ordered her five soldiers and her maidservants to take them back after they had been loaded onto carriages, and they did, covered by musket shot from the Castle. One of the cannon went off by accident as it was being moved and the terrified sailors ran away.

The first attack on Corfe came in early June 1643 by around 600 men on horse and foot. Led by Sir Walter Erle, Corfe was fired on from the nearby church and the surrounding hillsides. The artillery made little or no impact on Corfe's great walls, but all the same they requested Corfe surrender, Lady Mary refused. She was informed that no quarter would be given, that is; every man, woman and child inside Corfe, would be killed. This just hardened her resolve to fight on.

On the misty morning of 23rd June they returned, hoping to find the Castle willing to surrender. They had brought cannon, two six pounders and other armoury. They also brought a siege engine. Lady Mary's daughters sniped on the soldiers who were trying to work the siege engine, most of their bodies were protected by the woodwork, so the girls aimed for and hit their knees and lower legs, as the soldiers fell they got entangled in the ropework and had to limp away as best as they could.

Sir Walter Erle was wearing a bearskin coat to protect himself from getting shot and, when he felt in danger, he would crawl about on all fours. As it was summer he must have been very hot, but what did that matter when he was giving the soldiers inside Corfe a good laugh?

Lady Bankes took it upon herself to defend the upper ward of the castle with her daughters, maidservants, and her five soldiers. They heaved red hot embers and stones over the battlements to deter the scaling ladders. Once again the ladies sniped on the enemy soldiers with their muskets.

When she heard that Prince Maurice was nearing Blandford, Lady Mary sent an urgent message for help to defend Corfe. Prince Maurice sent Captain Robert Lawrence with around 80 men to add to her tiny garrison.

When the Parliamentarians heard the King's forces were on their way, they had had enough, and it was said "they ran away crying". Corfe had been saved for now. Sadly Lady Mary's husband never returned to Corfe, and she wasn't going to see him again as he died in December 1644 whilst in Oxford with the King.

For a short while there was peace at Corfe. It wasn't until December 1645 that Lady Mary Bankes found herself under attack again. Sir Thomas Fairfax sent a regiment of horse and two of foot to take the Castle, but the determined Lady Mary managed to hold out until February of the next year.

The death knell for Corfe was having a traitor in their midst. It finally fell on the 27th February 1646 with the help of one of her own officers, a turncoat called Lieutenant Colonel Pitman who was "weary of the Kings service".

Pitman, pretending he was going to fetch re-inforcements, immediately contacted the enemy on another pretence. He wanted to arrange an exchange for his brother, who was a parliamentarian prisoner. The beseigers entered Corfe on yet another pretence, that of being the Royalist re-enforcements under a Royalist flag and disguised as a Royalist regiment.

Many of the soldiers were local men who knew Corfe well and managed to get to strategic places in the castle during the invasion such as the towers and walkways.

It all happened by stealth, there were no casualties, it was agreed that everyone's lives would be spared. Lady Mary and her children were allowed to leave, and she was given the keys of Corfe to keep. She lived until 1661, brave even to the moment of her death. She did not tell her son she was ill and concealed her pain, she died on his wedding day, after attending the wedding.

Cromwell had the insolent Corfe slighted, a strange word to use, because there was nothing slight about the destruction of Corfe Castle. I took my son to see it when he was about nine, he looked at the drunken towers leaning at the gateway and the crumbling walls.

He stared at me - "Who did this mummy?" he asked.
"Cromwell and Colonel Dalbier with an awful lot of gunpowder I guess." I answered. Surprisingly he started to cry, "How could they do this to such a lovely castle? They must have been very bad men."
"Well, dear," I took his hand, "that depends on what side you're on."

Corfe Castle as it looks today (xxxv)

The Verney Women

Claydon House as it looks today (xxxvi)

Claydon House in Buckinghamshire, stands four square and regal overlooking pretty park land with a lake, sheep graze peacefully on the hillside much as they would have done in the time of the Civil War. The only change being the electric wire fence that stops them wandering onto the gravel path and the National Trust car park under the trees before the entrance gate.

During the English Civil War, Sir Edmund Verney, was famous for being the King's Standard bearer in the battle of Edgehill, where his hand was cut off as he refused to give up the King's Flag. A matter of honour.

It is the Verney women that I am going to write about, no they didn't go into battle, or dress as men, nor did they defend Claydon House from being beseiged. They just had to live through a war which divided their family in two, marriages arranged by their father, Sir Edmund and their eldest brother, Sir Ralph.

What follows is a short story of each of the sisters everyday lives.

Margaret Denton married Sir Edmund Verney on 14th December 1612, and throughout their marriage she was his "Dear Puss." She bore him twelve children, six of which were girls.

There is a mysterious portrait in Claydon which shows Dear Puss, in a very personal way, she is in a state of undress, with her hair long and loose. She is leaning her head on her hand exposing an arm which is red and scarred. It used to be called "the burnt arm portrait", but now it is thought it is no longer a burn, but a form of excema. What I think Margaret Verney is doing, is saying to her husband that I am not going to hide anything from you.
She had gone to great lengths to hide the scars when alive, and left details in her will how she should be covered when dead. It's therefore ironic that after all her care to hide her disfigurement, that her portrait is now on the wall in Claydon for all to see. She looks sad and exhausted in the portrait, hardly surprising as by the time this was painted she was only 27 years old and had already given birth to 8 children.

Margaret Verney was only 46 years old when she died in London in 1641. Her husband Edmund and her son Ralph were at her side. Margaret left a large family, her youngest Betty was only seven, leaving the girls without a mother made them troublesome. They spent a lot of time at their Grandmother Denton's house at Hillesden where they were spoilt by her and their Nurse Nan Fudd.

Sir Edmund never married again, Dear Puss, was his only love and on Sunday, 23rd of October 1642 just a year later he joined her. He did not die as she did, of a mysterious illness that lasted a few months, but in the first battle of the English Civil War at Edgehill.

He was the King's Standard Bearer, and surrounded by the enemy he took part in some violent hand to hand fighting. Killing one man and accounting for another by using his flag pole as a pike and spearing him through his body.

Brave Sir Edmund was outnumbered and went down. His grip on the King's standard was so tight, that the only way to get it out of his hand was to hack his hand off with it. Sir Edmund's body was never found, and the legend goes that the ghostly Sir Edmund within weeks, was trawling the battlefield looking for his hand. He has also been seen at Claydon searching the rooms. The Verney ring with the miniature portrait of Charles I was returned to Claydon after Edgehill, but the hand and Sir Ralph are still missing.

Luckily I had the opportunity some time ago to be shown around Broughton Castle by Lord & Lady Saye & Sele themselves. The 17th Century Saye & Seles were Roundheads, and they took me up to show me the room where battles had been plotted. They just happened to mention that Ralph Verney was still wearing the Verney ring when he came to dinner with them that week. Baronet Ralph Verney died in 2001. The ring is still with the Verney family.

Sir Edmunds and Margaret's daughters were left with just their eldest brother the new Sir Sir Ralph and their aged Grandmother to look out for them. Sometimes their Aunts tried to help, but were ignored by the girls. I can imagine the phrase “Don't tell me what to do, you're not my mother,” being used quite a lot.

The girls were Susan born on 18th April 1621, Penelope, affectionately known as Pen, born on 19th June 1622, Margaret (Peg) born 30th September, 1623, Cary, 28th December 1626, Mary, born 14th April 1628, and Elizabeth (Betty) born 12th September 1633. All the Verney girls survived into adulthood.

The boys were sent to school and abroad to be educated, but all Sir Edmund wanted from his daughters was that they could sing and dance, play an instrument, write a little, read a little French and be obedient. To get his daughters married would cost a dowry of £1000 each. Sir Edmund had no money, he was a true Cavalier, always living above his income. But he did have a son of marriageable age, and he had heard of a particularly wealthy young woman who had just come on to the marriage market, and this was how Mary Blacknall became Mary Verney.

Mary Verney, nee Blacknall possibly pregnant and holding her hand across her bump.(xxxvii)

Mary was married to Sir Ralph for her money, but they were in the fortunate position of actually loving one another. She was his Mischief and he was her Dearest Rogue.

Sir Ralph abandoned his sisters at Claydon to run abroad with his new wife. He had been voted a delinquent and removed from the House of Commons. His estate had been sequestered as he had been absent for 3 years. He wanted his estate back and asked for help from his uncle Dr William Denton. Uncle Dr told him that many women were pleading on behalf of their husbands for their estates.

"Women were never so useful as now".

Ralph Verney, the son,was a Parliamentarian whereas Sir Edmund his father was a Royalist serving the King. The only thing they both had in common was their large family and Claydon House, both of which had to be protected.

So a pregnant Mary sailed from Dieppe in Nov 1646 on her husband's behalf. She waded through the red tape and looked for influencial people who could help them, she tried Lady Warwick the parliamentarian wife of the Earl of Warwick, but she didn't offer to help.

Mary had what could have been flu over Christmas, it was January before she got rid of the temperature.
Paraphrased from the Early Modern English.

"It has brought me so low, that I can't walk twice the length of my chamber,and I am so depressed, I am almost ready to burst."

she said to Ralph in a letter.
She was waiting for a certificate from Buckingham committee's new officials, who were making life difficult for her by referring it to the House of Commons.

It took until June and by this time Mary was very near to having her baby, and on the 3rd of June she gave birth to a "lusty boy". In the middle of the tumult of the aftermath of war. It took her a long time to recover from the birth and it was August before she actually got to see Claydon again.

The house had billeted soldiers over the years they had been away,and the linen was in rags, what the rats hadn't eaten the military had destroyed. The only good thing about going to Claydon was that Mary was re-united with her seven year old son Jack, who followed her about like a puppy from the moment she arrived.

Mary had no good opinion of her sisters-in-law. As far as she was concerned she was glad that at least four of them were married, and hopefully no longer a burden to her husband, Sir Ralph. She believed that her sisters-in-law had been helping themselves to Claydon's linen and furniture, so she and the steward Will Roades made inventories of what was left and tried to find a safe place for what little valuables that were still in the house.

Mary decided to leave the new baby Ralph, with his brother Jack in the care of Nan Fudd and go back to London to try and finish her business. In October Mary was hit with the news that baby Ralph had died of convulsions, and at same time, her 9 year old daughter Pegg had died from fever and dysentery in France.

It was too much for Mary and she collapsed and cried for two days and nights.

When a Puritan husband cried for the loss of his 3 year old little girl, he was reminded by his wife, that their daughter had gone to a better place, and that some of their children were just "borrowed" from God for a short while and had to go back to Heaven, while others stayed to help them.

Even while coping with the death of her children, Mary still had the job she had been sent to do by Ralph to finish. Eventually Lady Warwick did help by sending her husband to the sequestation hearing, but only because Mary had pestered her nearly every day for a week.

The business was not yet over, Mary had to settle with all Ralph's debtors, and write thank you letters to everyone who had helped her. She also did some shopping, buying Ralph a new suit

> *"because I know you will weare any rusty old thing rather than bestow a new one upon yourselfe."*

Men don't change much, do they really?
But now she was just happy to be on her way back to her beloved "dearest Rogue". Mary and Ralph were only re-united for a short while in April.

Mary wasn't well, the exhaustion of the trip, the birth of her child, the heartbreak of losing two children at the same time, and the illness at Christmas that had knocked her for six, had taken it's toll. Mary died aged 34 in the Spring of 1650 leaving Ralph with their remaining children and his uncontrollable sisters.

Ralph was heartbroken, most young men would have re-married when the years' mourning period was over. Especially with a young family and an estate to run.

Ralph never re-married, saying no-one could ever take the place of Mary, she was the best of wives, she took care of his business with all the care she could. She was good, patient and kind, she helped him carry his burdens of his many troubles.

Sir Ralph lived on for a further 50 years without Mary, and had to learn to carry his many burdens alone.

Here are the stories of Ralph's sisters starting with Susan Verney. Susan was the eldest daughter and she was not obedient, after an argument with her parents, she was exiled to her Grandmother's house at Hillesden. She was desperately unhappy there, and her brother Mun (short for Edmund) tried to patch things up for her, telling his older brother Ralph that she was ashamed and frightened to tell her parents how miserable she was.

On the 5th August 1646 at the age of 25 Susan married Richard Alport, a widower. He had no children from his first marriage, and was so poor that Susan started her married life with him in the Fleet prison where he had been incarcerated for debt. They lived in the Fleet for two years.

Susan herself had already spent 8 days in prison,when her Grandmother's house had been sequestered by Parliament. So she was not too alarmed, she knew she was settling for what she could get, as she believed herself to be plain and thought that no other man would want her. The man she got was a kind loving man who did want her, and they married eventually.

Eventually, because her brother Ralph negotiated with Richard's creditors for nearly two years, haggling over her £1000 dowry that her father Sir Edmund had already spent before his death. Refusing to pay her debts and finally arguing the dowry down to £200 a year, and only settling in the end as Susan was pregnant. Unfortunately she lost the baby probably through stress.

They married at the start of August and Susan declared herself "never so happy as I am now." But childbirth was to rob her and her husband of any happiness they might have had, after two stillbirths and a very difficult pregnancy she gave birth crying in pain "Now, I thank God I am delivered." She called for her husband to come and kiss her. The child only lived for about an hour and Susan followed her child to the grave at midnight.

Penelope Verney married John Denton, her cousin on her mothers side at the beginning of November 1646. Not the most promising of starts,as John Denton of Fawler in Oxfordshire was well known as a drunk, but he swore he had it under control. He was an eager suitor and Pen was an eager wife to be. Already, to use current terms, getting past her sell by date. Age was not on her side she was now 26 and the marriage went ahead without Sir Ralph's approval. But her brother was only to happy once he found out,to have another sister settled and with only a slight increase to her £40 a year allowance.

Pen's marriage was not the happiest, John Denton married her for her money, enough money to drink. He was often violent towards her and quite often, to use her own words

"did kick me about the house."

Pen decided to give as good as she got, and after a big family get together at Claydon, they both went to board the coach back to London from Aylesbury. It was raining hard and Denton tried to push Pen out of the way to get an inside seat when she punched him hard in the face and took the seat. He had to ride outside the coach in the pouring rain with a black eye! Much to the amusement of his friends.

In November 1663 John Denton suddenly dropped dead to the relief of his wife and all her relatives, although Sir Ralph suggested to Pen that it might be a plan to

"Conceal his faults."

Denton's faults were well known, so it was really not necessary.

Pen and her favourite brother Henry (pet name Harry) moved in together to Pen's house in Covent Garden. They had always got on well together, Harry trained and rode his own race horses as there were no such thing as professional jockeys in 17th century England.

Harry fell sick in 1662 and his illness lasted till the Summer of 1671, Pen called in one of the best doctors of the day. The Oxford Physician Thomas Willis, but Harry was going downhill fast. Uncle Doctor, William Denton had just arrived back from a trip just in time to visit Harry and predict he had only 48 hours to live. He was right. Harry died after exactly 48 hours, leaving his favourite sister his fortune of over 700 guineas.*
In later life Pen married Sir John Osborne, a wealthy Irish Knight and had an apartment in Whitehall, and was happy at last.

Pen had no children with either of her husbands, perhaps John Denton's "kicking her about the house", had put paid to any hopes of motherhood she might have had. Before she died, she requested she be buried next to her favourite brother Harry (Henry Verney) in the Vault at Claydon, after all her adventures, all she wanted was to go home.

Margaret (Peg) Verney was born in January 1639 at her grandmother's house Hillesden, with the same upbringing as her sisters, but with a small inheritance of £1000 from her Aunt Eure, which her brother Ralph had tied up so tight, she could not really get her hands on it. His idea was that it would provide an income for her until she married. A young man was "bought" for her with the help of her brothers Henry and Ralph. Although Henry seemed to want to take all the credit for it. Peg was 22 when she went to live with her husband Thomas Elmes in Covent Garden.

Thomas had a jealous temper, and the young Peg was far away from Claydon and help. As Thomas' temper grew shorter, he became more violent towards her. After two years her sister Susan noticed a change in her,

> *"Poor Peg has married a very humoursome cross boy, she is very much altered for the worse since she was married, because he makes her cry day and night."*

* *a guinea is a pound and a shilling.*

Sometimes Thomas was jealous and violent and at other times very loving. However, he was unable to stay calm for very long, Peg's brother Henry tried to mediate between them, and sometimes managed to calm Thomas for the moment by using "long words". But brother Henry could not live in Covent Garden to protect her, so Peg was left to the mercy of Thomas Elmes' rage. Elmes left Peg in 1648 and travelled to France supposedly to enter a monastry, which in the end he didn't do.

On his return, he tried to reconcile with Peg, but it didn't work things were worse, so they agreed to separate and Peg went to live with her sister Cary, leaving poor Sir Ralph trying to get enough money out of Elmes for Peg to live on.

Cary Verney was fifteen in 1642, when her father Sir Edmund was in throes of arranging her marriage, Cary liked his choice of man, a Royalist officer, Thomas Gardiner, a Captain of Horse from Cuddesdon in Oxfordshire. By the end of July Cary was a Gardiner and living at her husband's family home at Cuddesdon,

"taking his sisters as my sisters"

and his grandmother

"as my grandmother."

Fitting in as well as she could amongst strangers, whose only expectation of her, was to provide Thomas with a male heir.

After a honeymoon period of two weeks, Thomas left Cary to join King Charles and his army at York. Cary missed him, he had been a good husband to her, now he was two hundred miles away, and she was worried for him. She was also worried for her new family, although the war had not properly started yet, everyone was preparing for it. Cary had heard Parliament troops had pillaged the Oxford colleges and were likely to pillage the country as they moved through it.

At Claydon, preparations were being made to protect the house, Will Roades the Verney's steward, was already on the alert. Two men at the closed doors during the day, all the doors locked at night and muskets and balls ready to fend off any attackers after the riches inside the house. War was coming to England. Sir Edmund had stood by the King reluctantly as he said "I do not like the quarrel." But Sir Ralph, the heir to Claydon was for the Parliament wanting "peace and liberty."

Cary, I'm sure just wanted her new husband back. In July 1645 Captain Thomas Gardiner was shot dead in a skirmish outside Oxford, leaving Cary a pregnant widow at the age of just eighteen. She was distraught, her in-laws refused to pay for her keep, the widows jointure. Worst of all as far as the Gardiners were concerned, she gave birth to a girl, so she was thrown out without a penny. Cary returned with her young daughter to the safe haven of Claydon. Perhaps it was for the best, because if she had provided the Gardiners with a heir, they may have kept the boy to bring up themselves, and Cary would have been completely alone. For a family that she had so completely adopted as her own to treat her in this way is abominable.

Seven years later Cary, who was then 26, met and married John Stewkeley. He was a good natured widower with four teenage children. They lived in his country estate Preshaw near Winchester. Along with her Gardiner daughter and John's teenage brood, the family became larger when Cary gave birth to John junior, quickly followed by six more sons. Their marriage was a happy one, but Cary refused to change her name, keeping herself as Lady Gardiner for the rest of her life. She had been married to a Knight and she saw no reason to give up the status that brought her. Probably because it annoyed the rest of the Gardiner family and that was a good enough reason on it's own.

Cary died in October 1704 and was buried next to her husband of many years John Stewkeley at Bray in Berkshire.

Mary (Mall) Verney, was born as the penultimate daughter of Sir Edmund and Margaret on 14th April 1628. Mall was probably the most independent of the Verney girls, also the most wild. When she was 26 she was living in London with her maid, as a single women on £10 a quarter supplied to her by her brother Ralph. Mall liked men, liked flirting, and quite often got herself into trouble by having so many admirers spend time with her. None of her men friends however, wanted to marry her.

A quick aside here on the difference in morals of 17th Century men and women, women were not allowed to have lovers or extra marital affairs. But if a wife found out her husband was playing around she was told to ignore it, it may be a phase, and that if it didn't end after a year or so, ignore it, because the man would never change.

Prince Rupert of the Rhine had many mistresses and many children by them, all daughters. When asked why he never married any of them he replied:

> *"If one treads in a cowpat, one does not wear it on one's head for all the world to see."*

Men could do as they liked, but women had to protect their reputation. Mall's reputation was dissolving, in August 1654, she told her Uncle Doctor Denton, that she was sure she had dropsy. Being a doctor he was sure she was pregnant, but he gave her some medicine just in case.

Pregnancy was a downward spiral unless a husband could be found. Young women could buy physics and potions made of a herb called Rue, that "would cleanse the womb." But sometimes it would not work, and the pregnancy would be hidden until birth, many a newborn would take it's first and last breaths in the dank darkness of a deep well.

When Mall's pregnancy was confirmed Uncle Doctor said to Sir Ralph:- (Paraphrased from the original.)

> *"I am at my wits end,I do not know what to do or say. Mall is facing shame, imprisonment, beggary, she has no money to dress a child, all her friends will alienate her, and I want foremost to express the ugliness of it towards God and Man."*

The family were beside themselves, fornication was a sin, and who was the father? There were three suspects, Colonel McShane, Charles Goode, or Robin Lloyd, the Colonel was from a respectable family and Mall's sister Cary was hoping that they were already secretly married. If not Charles Goode might take Mall for the right price. Cary hoped it was not Robin Lloyd who was an apothecary's messenger.

As it turned out it was Lloyd's child, and Mall had already taken certain arrangements into her own hands. She and Lloyd had committed a criminal offence under the law of 1650 which was brought in to suppress incest,fornication, and adultery. So she had tried to arrange a brothel keeper who would farm out the baby when it was born, but she wanted payment for her help.

Mall could not return to the safety of Claydon to have the child, it would be a scandal that would ruin the Verney's reputation in the county. So in the comparative anonimity of London, Mall wrote to her brother Sir Ralph to ask for £20 to be "cured" of her illness. In it she agreed to be sent away (Ireland or Barbados were mentioned) if that was what he wanted. She ended her desperate letter to Ralph

"end me or mend me."

Robin, the father had also had thoughts on the matter, he asked his brother Frank and his wife to take on the child and they agreed. Mall gave birth to a healthy boy in November 1654. Already Mall was changing her mind, she didn't want to leave London and suggested moving nearer to Cary.

Cary did not want this scandal on her doorstep, of all the family Cary was the most shocked at the situation. Cary herself had been a woman alone with a child, but she had been married decently to a man she loved. Mall as far as she was concerned was a delinquent.

The plan was for Mall to stay in London until the end of February with Sir Ralph paying for her keep. When the child was handed over to Frank and his wife she was to leave London. Sir Ralph would let her know where he had decided to put her.

But Mall wanted to marry Robin, and use her brother's money to do it. Sir Ralph was furious, after all his help, she was throwing it back in his face. He cut her off without a penny and told her sisters not to help her.

Mall was penniless and starving, living hand to mouth on credit. She wrote and told Sir Ralph that his dogs ate better than she did and she would be glad of their food. He gave in to Mall in June 1655 and resumed her payments, part of the money was being held back to pay her creditors, and she was not allowed to have any advances on her cash.

Naughty Mall could not behave even when saved from starvation. She married Robin Lloyd on 2nd November 1655. Sir Ralph was so furious he never spoke her name again, calling her "the unfortunate party." Deceived yet again, he only ever wrote to her through an intermediary called Mr Gape. She and Robin emigrated to Wales, Robin's homeland, where it was cheaper to live and where she gave birth to another child.

Sir Ralph continued to support Mall financially until her death in 1684, but he never wanted to see or speak to her again.

Elizabeth (Betty) Verney, was born the youngest daughter in 1633. She was a spoilt and petulant little girl, who seemed to do as she liked in Claydon, and threw tantrums when she didn't get her way. Sir Ralph's wife Mary didn't like her at all

"She is a pestilent wench, much the worst natured and willfullest of them all."

The teenage Betty was uncontrollable, proud, cross and lazy. She demanded expensive clothes and was rude and obnoxious. She was passed amongst her sisters, none of whom could cope with her, and despite threatening to kill herself she was sent to a private school in London that Uncle Doctor Denton found for her. This at least improved her manners and when Uncle Doctor visited her he could hardly believe the change in the girl in such a short amount of time.

Betty was the least written about of all the Verney girls, and all I could find was that she had a lot in common with Mall, she married below her, a clergyman called Adams, while pregnant with his child. The baby died. But she gave birth to a daughter she called Peg, who went to live at Claydon with Sir Ralph to help her recover from an illness. Betty had really sent her to escape the poverty at home,and hopefully find a place in life. Betty lived as the poor widow of a Clergyman for over forty years. She returned to Claydon with Cary while Sir Ralph was dying and wrote to his son Jack, to tell him how his father was. She stayed for Sir Ralph's burial in the Verney Vault.

Betty died a few months after her brother, and is buried with her husband in Bray.

There is so much to say about these women, the more I looked the more I found. During the Civil War at Hillesden when the house was sequestered by Parlimentarians and raised to the ground they were stripped to their shifts and thrown out of their grandmother's house. Only their brother's Parliamentarian leanings saved them from a worse fate.

Out of this horror came came a strange romance, Uncle Alexander Denton's sister Susan fell in love with the Parliament Captain that destroyed her home Captain Jeremiah Abercrombie. It was love at first sight for both of them, but the Captain was killed the following year and buried amongst his in-laws in the churchyard at Hillesden.

While almost at the same time Alexander Denton's daughter Margaret, married Colonel William Smith who led the defence of Hillesden.

Truly a family by the sword divided.

The Verney Tomb in Claydon Church (xxxviii)

17th Century Recipes

A 17c Summer Feast (xxxix)

As today every family had their own recipes for the food they eat, much like our own recipes today. Take the well loved favourite Spaghetti Bolognese, although there is a "proper" recipe, everyone's version is slightly different. Some-one will add corn for example, others will leave out garlic, or put in mushrooms. For us today, it's all about taste, trend, likes and dislikes and allergy awareness.

For a woman in the 17th Century, it's all about what you could get your hands on at the time of year,what you had preserved,what you could afford, and perhaps what your husband could catch.

In the photograph above you will see my version of a 17th Century Summer Feast. Set out as if for Feast day.

There are apples some will be last year's crop, saved and wrapped and kept dry in the loft. There are a few oranges bought from Orange seller (Nell Gwyn actress favourite of Charles II was one). Orange drops, a kind of sticky marmalade sweet, fruit cake, home made bread and butter, cheddar cheese,(a lot of cheese would be a local variety) wild strawberries, very small but sweet. (Now called Alpine strawberries).To drink - small beer, a weak sweet beer watered down with lemon juice. (Think shandy!)

In the other tent over the fire there is a lamb stew with carrots and onions and turnips being cooked with a handful of herbs thrown in. Lovage, gives a very savoury meaty taste, same goes for Bay.

On the camp fires of the Army the Baggage women would cook any rabbits, chickens, fish or deer given to them without asking any questions about where they came from. Puddings would be boiled in gauze in a pot. There would be a spit turning for the meat, a hot fire for boiling, and hot ashes would be raked out to give the opportunity to simmer or fry.

Once when at Huntingdon I was attending a rather smoky fire which made my eyes run with water, and burnt the sleeve of my bodice with a spark, a member of the public came up and asked if the fire was a real fire or a hologram!

Here are some real 17th Century Recipes for you to try.

How to Make Ye Sassage meat

Take a little of ye lean of veal and a little sueit & sage leaves a small quanititie of tyme and winter savory and a little lean of bacon. Chop all this very small yn put it to ye yelks of 2 eggs and season with nutmeg pepper and salt.

1lb veal, 3 rashers streaky bacon, 2 small egg yolks, sage thyme and winter savoury if available, chopped finely, seasoning.

Mince the meat and season, add the egg yolks (do not make the mixture too wet) and mix in the herbs. Shape into sausage shapes or flat patties. Cover with flour and fry in butter.

Orange Cakes (orange sweets)

Take ye fairest oranges you can get and cut ym in quart & take out their insides&put itt into a basin, and take out all ye seeds and skins very clean and pare ye rinds as you can ye length of ye Oranges set them over ye fire in fair water and boyl them till they are tender,yn take them up and mince ym small & take ye weight of double refind sugar & boil ym to a Candy height,ym take it off the fire& put ye rindss and ye insides and ye sugar all together and set it over a fire to boyl a little and stir it when it comes offe, yn set it offe in a stobe in an Earthern basin, keep fire to it, till it be fit to drop,yn drop them on glasses and them dry thereon.

4 Oranges, Sugar.

Take the skin off the oranges very thinly and boil it for ten minutes until tender. Take the pith off the oranges by pouring boiling water over them and leaving them a few minutes, then they'll peel easily. Quarter and slice up the oranges taking out any skin, pips pith etc.

When the peel is tender, drain off the water and weigh the cooked peel. Measure out the same weight in sugar.

Chop the peel very finely and put in with the sugar. Stir over a low heat until the sugar has melted, then boil hard until it starts to turn brown and caramelise. Add the orange flesh and continue to boil, mashing and stirring until the liquid has evaporated and the mixture is thick.

Drop small spoonfuls onto greased baking tray and dry in the bottom of a warm oven.

Makes about 12 cakes - they look like flat circles of marmalade - well mine did, and they lasted about 12 seconds when the troops got their hands on them!

To make a Posset
There are many many Posset recipes, every family had their own.
Some used cream in the alchohol, some added herbs. But this is mine.
Warm a cup of milk until almost boiling, add two teaspoons of sugar and a tablespoon of whiskey,stir in and drink, helps sleep.

17th Century Recipes for Beauty

A very good wash for ye face
2 ounces of pearl barley to 3 pints of water, boil it till it comes to a quart, then put it to a Spoonfull of Brandy and half a dram
of Camphire and one Lemon.
2oz of Pearl Barley (60g)
3 pints (one and a half litres of water)
1 tablespoon of Brandy
Juice of one lemon
A few drops of camphor oil.
Boil the pearl barley rapidly in water for 10 - 15 minutes until the water has reduced by a third. Strain into a bowl and add the brandy, lemon juice and camphor. Allow it to cool down.
The pearl barley softens the skin, and the lemon tightens it, a good recipe if you are feeling tired.

But remember even in the 17th Century it was advised that the best way to keep your looks is to laugh more and worry less!

As white skin is more attractive, use lemon juice on freckles to reduce their appearance, and pox scars can be filled with a paste made of flour and paper, but not until they are healed.

17th Century Recipes for Cures

For a pain in ye stomack in young folks
Rost 2 cevill oranges and put ym into some saffron then rost ym and steep ym in a quart of white wine and Drink half a pint each morning and walk after it till it doe goode.
2 Seville oranges (or two large sweet oranges
2 pints (1 litre) white wine
Saffron
Cut the oranges in half and sprinkle with saffron.
Bake in a moderate oven for 15-20 minutes then steep the oranges overnight in the white wine. Strain into a bottle and drink every morning until cured.
Tastes lovely but saffron can purge so beware!

For a Sore Throat
Tak powder of Ginger and mix it with Brandy, stiff enuff to spreed on a Cloth and put it to the throat put a peice of Muslen betwen or it will draw it out in pimpels
1 teaspoon ground ginger
2 tablespoons of brandy
Mix together to form a paste spread on a cloth and wrap around the throat.
Acts as an effective counter - irritant.

17th Century Women's Names

What would your name have been? (xxxx)

The most popular womans names in England in the 17th Century were:

1. Elizabeth (e.g Elizabeth Cromwell)
2. Mary (e.g Charles 1st daughter)
3. Ann or Anne (as in Anne Dymock)
4. Jane (as in Jane Lane)
5. Margaret (Margaret Newcastle)
6. Dorothy (a Quaker name)
7. Alice (believed to have come from Germany)
8. Isobel (the Spanish version of Elizabeth)
9. Catherine (the French version of Katherine)
10. Jennet (English common name)

Some 17th Century Surnames

- Aymes, Aubrey, Austin
- Bennett, Beauchamp, Bowyer
- Capel, Cooper, Cromwell
- Denton, Dudley, Dutton
- Erskin, Essex, Evans
- Fortescue, Framlingham, Foulke (Fawkes)
- Gascoyne, Grey, Griffith
- Harbottle, Hastings, Hopkin
- Jervaise, Jones
- Kelly, Kenelm, Kildare
- Langdale, Lennox, Le Strange
- Mandeville, Marmion, Mildmay
- Norton, Norris
- Owen
- Pontesbury,Popham
- Radcliffe, Randal, Redmain
- Sackville, Seymor, Sidney
- Talbot, Thorp, Timothy
- Usher, Underwood
- Verney, Vesey, Villiers,
- Warwick, Worth, Wycomb
- Young
- Zouche

There are more surnames, but I thought these were interesting, if anyone finds an English surname beginning with X please let me know!

Puritan Names

The Puritans wanted names that had nothing to do with the Catholic church. Puritans fought in the English Civil War against what they thought was a King heavily influenced by his Catholic wife. Because of this some left the country to start a new life by colonising America, to them the New World, giving names to their towns after the places they had left, adding "new" in front of them, such as New York and New England.

They chose their names to remind themselves of their religious life, sometimes they used Hebrew names from the Bible, and sometimes they chose virtues they'd like their children to have. It was a way of telling Puritan children from their neighbours. Sometimes the names they chose were just downright weird, but that is only my humble opinion. Here we are then, Puritan names. They seem to be for boys or girls except the obvious ones like Truth, Faith, Verity, Prudence, anything that they thought a girl ought to be.

- Abednego, Amity, Ashes,
- Balthazar, Barebones,Bathsheba, Bestedfast,
- Constance, Continent, Creedence, Desire, Dust,
- Ephrahim
- Fear-God, Farewell,Felicity, Foresaken, Freegift,
- Handmaid, Happy, Humiliation, Hephzibah,Hope, Hopestill,
- Jolly,
- Liberty,
- Placidia,Prudence,
- Tace(means be quiet),Tenacious,Trinity,
- Vanity, Verity.

As women and men are usually connected, and as most women are nosey, here are the most common first names of men of the time.

The Top Ten Men's Names of the 17th Century

1. John
2. William
3. Thomas
4. Edward
5. James
6. Henry
7. Robert
8. Richard
9. Francis
10. George

Note: For all the Andrews in the Sealed Knot, and there are many - they would have been called Andreas or Drew. Not Andy.

The World Turned Upside Down

A broadside ballad written after the English Civil War that describes how life changed for the people of England.

Listen to me and you shall hear,
news hath not been this thousand year:
Since Herod, Caesar, and many more,
you never heard the like before.
Holy-dayes are despis'd, new fashions are devis'd.
Old Christmas is kicked out of Town

Yet let's be content, and the times lament,
you see the world turn'd upside down.

The wise men did rejoyce to see our Savior Christs Nativity:
The Angels did good tidings bring,
the Sheepheards did rejoyce and sing.
Let all honest men, take example by them.
Why should we from good Laws be bound?

Yet let's be content, and the times lament,
you see the world turn'd upside down.

Command is given, we must obey,
and quite forget old Christmas day:
Kill a thousand men, or a Town regain,
we will give thanks and praise amain.
The wine pot shall clinke, we will feast and drinke.
And then strange motions will abound.

Yet let's be content, and the times lament,
you see the world turn'd upside down.

Our Lords and Knights, and Gentry too,
doe mean old fashions to forgoe:
They set a porter at the gate,
that none must enter in thereat.
They count it a sin, when poor people come in.
Hospitality it selfe is drown'd.

Yet let's be content, and the times lament,
you see the world turn'd upside down.

The serving men doe sit and whine,
and thinke it long ere dinner time:
The Butler's still out of the way,
or else my Lady keeps the key,
The poor old cook, in the larder doth look,
Where is no goodnesse to be found,

Yet let's be content, and the times lament,
you see the world turn'd upside down.

To conclude, I'll tell you news that's right,
Christmas was kil'd at Naseby fight,
Charity was slain at that same time,
Jack Tell troth too, a friend of mine,
Likewise then did die, rost beef and shred pie,
Pig, Goose and Capon no quarter found.

Yet let's be content, and the times lament,
you see the world turn'd upside down

BIBLIOGRAPHY

Suggested further reading

A Royal Passion The Turbulent Marriage of Charles I & Henrietta-Maria by Katie Whitaker ISBN 978-0-8609-8 Orion Books.

By The Sword Divided Eyewitness Accounts of the English Civil War by John Adair ISBN 0-7509-1858-6 Sutton Publishing.

Elizabeth of the Sealed Knot by Doreen Cripps ISBN 0-900093-43-9 Roundwood Press (currently out of print)

Handbook of Herbs growing/cooking/health etc by Margot McLeod SBN 7160-06251-1 Elliot Right Way Books

Mad Madge Margaret Cavendish Duchess of Newcastle, Royalist Writer & Romantic by Katie Whitaker. IBSN 0-99-28484 Vintage

Original Country Recipes from a Dorset family cookery book of the 17th century by Mary Chafin ISBN 0-333-27381-8 Macmillan

The English Civil War Day by Day by Wilfred Emberton ISBN 1-84013-003-2 Sutton Publishing (currently out of print

The Verneys a True Story of Love, War, and Madness in 17th Century England by Adrian Tinniswood ISBN 978-0-224-07255-7

The Weaker Vessel Woman's Lot in 17th Century England by Lady Antonia Fraser ISBN 0-297-78381-5 Orion Publishing

Women All on Fire The Women of the English Civil War by Alison Plowden ISBN 0-7509-3765-3 Sutton Publishing

The Robe May 1667 IBSN 978-1-905686-85-8

The Stuart Press at 117 Farleigh Road, Backwell, Bristol. Produce many reference paperbacks and are well worth a look , as they give in depth historical information on the period.

List of Illustrations

Image Craigy144: Public Domain

Oliver Cromwell - Elizabeth's "Old one." (viii)

Margaret Evans: 2015: All rights reserved

Hester Tradescant and her children (ix)

Margaret Evans: 2012: All rights reserved

Tradescant's House, South Lambeth (from Tennant),

wood engraving, ca. 1883. (x)

Source: en.wikipedia.org/wiki/John_Tradescant_the_Younger#/media/File:Tradescant%27s_House,_South_Lambeth.png

image Moonraker: Public Domain

The Tradescant tomb in the gardens of

the Royal Horticultural Museum designed by Hester (xi)

Source: commons.wikimedia.org/wiki/File:Tradescant_tomb_-_geograph.org.uk_-_1140617.jpg

image Peter Barr [CC BY-SA 2.0 (http://creativecommons.org/licenses/by-sa/2.0)], via Wikimedia Commons

Lady Anne Cunningham Defender of Scotland (xii)

Image adapted and recoloured in 2015 from

http://www.thepeerage.com/p10940.htm

www.thepeerage.com/109400_001.jpg

copyright : unknown

Margaret Cavendish (xiii)

Portrait of Margaret Cavendish, Lady Newcastle, from the frontispiece to her 'Poems and Fancies', 1653

Artist: unknown

source: commons.wikimedia.org/wiki/File:MargaretCavendish.JPG

image: Public Domain

William Cavendish entertained King Charles and Queen Henrietta-Maria in this room at Bolsover Castle. (xiv)

Gonzales Coques, "Portrait of a married couple in a park," or 'Lord Cavendish and his wife Margaret in the Rubens Garden in Antwerp' 1662 (Kat.Nr. 858). Staatliche Museen zu Berlin, Gemäldegalerie;

Foto: Jörg P. Anders. (xv)

Bolsover Castle, Derbyshire Home of the Newcastles (xvi)

Lucy Hutchinson 1620-1681 (xvii)

Source:

en.wikipedia.org/wiki/Lucy_Hutchinson#/media/File:Lucy_Hutchinson_(1620-1681).jpg

image: unknown : Public Domain

Anne Fanshawe 1625-1680 (xviii)

artist: Cornelis Janssens van Ceulen

source: en.wikipedia.org/wiki/Ann,_Lady_Fanshawe#/media/File:Ann_Fanshawe_(1625-1680),_wife_of_Sir_Richard_Fanshawe.jpeg

image: MarmadukePercy : Public Domain

She-soldiers of the Sealed Knot marching off to fight in Nantwich (xix)

A mixed troupe of Sealed Knot Royalist and Roundhead Cavalry with the King in the centre (xx)

Ripley Castle (xxi)

The photograph above was taken at one of our Sealed Knot re-enactments at Newstead Abbey. The Cavalier behind the King with the red ostrich feather is a female showing how Lady Jane could disguise herself as a man. (xxii)

*Margaret Evans: Sherbourne 2014: *

Musket ball holes in Ripley Church (xxiii)

*Margaret Evans: Ripley Church 2013: *

Sealed Knot Lady drummers at Naseby Battlefield waiting to go on (xxiv)

*Margaret Evans: Naseby Battlefield 2014: *

Sarah Evans(Eyans) 1658 (xxv)

*Margaret Evans: Chastleton 2015: *

Arthur Jones of Chastleton House (xxvi)

*Margaret Evans: Chastleton 2015: *

The hidden room with door open, when the door is closed the tapestry completely obscures the entrance and it looks just like a wall. The carpet is upturned because my husband tripped over it taking photos! (xxvii)

*Margaret Evans: Chastleton 2015: *

Mary Frith the Roaring Girl (xxvii)

Image of Mary Frith from title page of The Roaring Girl

source : en.wikipedia.org/wiki/Mary_Frith#/media/File:Mollcutpurse.jpg

image Curtangel : Public Domain

Sealed Knot re-enactment where Women are acting as the Baggage train (xxix)

*Margaret Evans: Newstead Abbey 2012: *

Lady Brilliana Harley (xxx)

No known source: Public Domain

Charlotte Stanley, Countess of Derby (xxxi)

"Charlotte Countess derby" by Anthony Van Dyck (1599 - 1641) - Frick Collection, New York http://www.artble.com/artists/anthony_van_dyck/paintings/james_seventh_earl_of_derby_his_lady_and_child. Licensed under Public Domain via Wikimedia Commons - https://commons.wikimedia.org/wiki/File:Charlotte_Countess_derby.jpg#/media/File:Charlotte_Countess_derby.jpg

Part of Lathom House as it is today. (xxxii)

"Lathom House West Wing" by Small-town hero - Own work.

Licensed under Public Domain via Commons - https://commons.wikimedia.org/wiki/File:Lathom_House_West_Wing.JPG#/media/File:Lathom_House_West_Wing.JPG

Basing House by Wenceslaus Hollar (xxxiii)

"Wenceslaus Hollar - The Siege of Basing House" by Baigent, Francis Joseph & Millard, James Elwin (1889). - A history of the ancient town and manor of Basingstoke in the county of Southampton; with a brief account of the siege of Basing House, A. D. 1643-1645, page 427.

Licensed under Public Domain via Commons - https://commons.wikimedia.org/wiki/File:Wenceslaus_Hollar_-_The_Siege_of_Basing_House.jpg#/media/File:Wenceslaus_Hollar_-_The_Siege_of_Basing_House.jpg

A courage above her sex (xxxiv)

"Mary Bankes-Hawtry by Henry Pierce Bone, after John Hoskins" by Henry Pierce Bone - Christie's. Licensed under Public Domain via Commons - https://commons.wikimedia.org/wiki/File:Mary_Bankes-Hawtry_by_Henry_Pierce_Bone,_after_John_Hoskins.jpg#/media/File:Mary_Bankes-Hawtry_by_Henry_Pierce_Bone,_after_John_Hoskins.jpg

Corfe Castle as it looks today (xxxv)

Margaret Evans: Corfe Castle 2012: All rights reserved

Claydon House as it looks today (xxxvi)

Margaret Evans: Claydon House 2015: All rights reserved

Mary Verney, nee Blacknall possibly pregnant and holding her hand across her bump. (xxxvii)

Margaret Evans: 2010: All rights reserved

The Verney Tomb in Claydon Church (xxxviii)

Margaret Evans: Claydon Church 2015: All rights reserved

A 17c Summer Feast (xxxix)

Margaret Evans: East Hendred 2011: All rights reserved

What would your name have been? (xxxx)

Margaret Evans: Newstead Abbey 2012: All rights reserved

Printed in Great Britain
by Amazon